M Y S IN

A Bilingual Anthology of Poetry in Chinese and English
英語/漢語雙語詩集

我的罪

My sin

Author, Translator: Xi Nan

作者、翻譯： 西楠

Xi Nan (西楠), writes and translates, indie publisher of *Xi Nan & Fish Lu STUDIO, London*. She recently has been living and traveling in Africa with her life partner.

西楠，寫作，翻譯，*Xi Nan & Fish Lu STUDIO, London* 工作室獨立出版人。她近期和她的愛人旅居非洲。

Preface: Love and Truth, Two Central Themes in Xi Nan's Works

by Fish Lu

Xi Nan writes poetry, novels, and all kinds of works. She went to study abroad since her adolescence (in high school), and has been living there for a long time, that's why her life experience is more unique and complex than those of her peers in general. These are reflected in both Xi Nan's poems and novels. Xi Nan's works authentically reflect the realities of life, offering glimpses into the author's own experiences. Only with a profound sense of introspection and great courage, one could portray themes of truth. Love and truth, these two enduring motifs form the cornerstone of Xi Nan's works.

Xi Nan's writings focus on herself, exploring personal experiences and perspectives, with very few grand narratives. In some works, she assumes the role of a rebel (for example, in her family-related works)—I believe this portrayal does not capture the true essence of Xi Nan and is a deep misconception. I have some thoughts on this.

Generally speaking, rebellion is often associated with adolescence. As people get older and more experienced in life, most of them eventually choose to reconcile and conform to the ranks they once opposed. Not so with Xi Nan. Xi Nan's rebellion, both in her writings and in her life, has persisted to this day. It is distinct from the rebelliousness of adolescence, as it stems from a clash of values and a commitment to staying true to her inner convictions, even if it means diverging from social norms sometimes.

It seems to me that Xi Nan's image of a rebel comes, in part, from her unwavering honesty and relentless quest for truth. She doesn't rebel just for the sake of rebellion. However, when one is always 'naked' and placing him/herself in a world of falsehood, one inevitably becomes the epicenter of turmoil. This cannot be said to be unconnected with the bipolar disorder that developed in Xi Nan later.

Those who are familiar with Xi Nan's works and herself know that Xi Nan suffers from bouts of bipolar disorder, once even to a rather severe degree—a fact Xi Nan openly acknowledges without hesitation. While some may find it unsettling, Xi Nan remains committed to portraying it authentically in her works. She stays true to herself, and undoubtedly displaying profound introspection along the way.

Another important theme in Xi Nan's works is 'love', encompassing both the passionate love and desire shared between romantic lovers and the universal love that extends beyond individual connections. There is love that stems from primal human instincts as well as a profound love for humanity that transcends those instincts. Xi Nan has named this important poetry-collection of hers *My Sin*—this is surely the name of one of the poems, but it also shows Xi Nan's introspection and self-awareness when digging inward and deep in her soul. Eros represents the instinctive aspect of love, while romantic relationships have more beauty and pursuit in love, but a deeper level of love must be about self-awareness. There is a power of self-awareness in Xi Nan's works.

Authenticity alone may hold its own power, yet it can often feel cold. Love, however, emanates warmth and embraces, embodying the most exquisite and contagious aspect of human nature. The fusion of authenticity and love undoubtedly constitutes one of the most invaluable and virtuous qualities of humanity—this is also a fundamental theme in Xi Nan's works (especially in her poems), which runs through almost the entire time and field of her creations. While this can certainly be seen as the author's deliberate quest, it is also one of her inherent qualities.

I would like to emphasize again that in recent years, Xi Nan's works have shown more of a power of digging inwards and deeper. This is a kind of ability and strength of deep introspection. This transition in Xi Nan's writings moves from the instinctive expression and catharsis in the early years to a phase characterized by introspection and self-awareness. It is more evident in Xi Nan's recent poems, which have become more self-aware and rational. The change has happened, and is inevitable, which is undoubtedly a good change.

late summer ~ early autumn 2018, first draft in Wuhan, China
December 2020, revised in Zhejiang, China

(Fish Lu, the author of this article, is a poet, experimental writer, and co-indie-publisher of Xi Nan & Fish Lu STUDIO, London. He is also the life partner of Xi Nan, and they currently reside in Africa.)

序言：愛與真，西楠寫作中的兩大主題

文｜魯魚

西楠寫詩、小說，和各類文字，由於少年（高中時）就留學英國，後來長期在那里工作、生活，人生經歷相對一般的同齡人更多了一些獨特與復雜。這些在西楠的詩和小說裡都有所體現。西楠的作品比較真實，在作品裡或多或少都能看到作者的影子。真實，需要高度的自省，也需要巨大的勇氣。愛與真，是西楠作品裡兩大不變的主題。

西楠的創作專注於自身，鮮有宏大的敘事，在一些作品裡，她以反叛者的形像出現（例如在她的家庭題材作品中）。我想這不是真實的西楠，是一個深深的誤解。對此，我有一些思考。

一般而言，青春期的反叛更加常見。隨著年齡和生活閱歷的增加，大多數人最終都會選擇和解，回到他們曾經反對過的隊伍。而西楠不是。西楠在她的作品、甚至生活中的反叛，一直持續到現在。這肯定不能再與青春期的逆反相提並論。這裡邊既有價值觀的衝突，也有一個人想要葆有內心真實的願望，於是難免有時顯得和社會現實格格不入。

在我看來，西楠的反叛者形象，一定程度上正來源於：她自身的真實和對真實的不斷追尋。她並非是為反叛而反叛。可是，當一個人始終赤身裸體地將自己置身於普遍虛偽虛假的現實中，就無異於常常把自己置身於風暴中心。西楠後來患上精神躁鬱症，不能說與此無關。

熟悉西楠作品和她本人的，都知道西楠患有躁鬱症，甚至曾經達到一個比較嚴重的程度。這一點西楠自己也並不迴避。在一些人看來，這可能會給人有點血淋淋的感覺。但是西楠在她的作品中，仍力求真實的把它展現出來。這裡既有其本真的一面，也無疑有著她深刻的自省。

西楠作品中的另一個重要主題是，愛。這個愛，既是愛情、愛欲，也是普世之愛。有出於人類本能的愛，也有超越本能的人性之愛。西楠把自己這部重要的詩集起名為《我的罪》，這固然是其中一首詩的名字，但同時也表明了西楠向內、向靈魂深處挖掘的自省與自覺。愛欲是出乎本能的，愛情則多了一份美好與追求，而更深層次的愛，一定關乎自覺。西楠的作品裡有一種自覺的力量。

單純的真實並不缺乏力量，但難免冷冰冰的。而愛是有溫度的、溫暖的，也是人性裡最美好、最有感染力的部分。真與愛的相融相合無異是人類最難能可貴、最高貴的品質之一。這也是西楠作品中的基本主題，貫穿了她創作的幾乎全部時間和領域（特別在她的詩作中）。這固然可以說是作者的一種追求，但也有其天然品質的一面。

我想再強調一次，近幾年來西楠的作品裡更多的表現出了一種向內、向更深層次挖掘的力量。這是一種深刻自省的能力和力量。這也讓西楠的創作從早期更多的出乎本能的表達和宣洩，轉向了自省自覺的層面。這在西楠近期的詩裡表現更多，變的更加自覺和理性了。轉變已經發生，轉變無可避免，這無疑是一種好的轉變。

2018 年夏末秋初，初稿於中國武漢
2020 年 12 月，修訂於中國浙江

（本文作者魯魚系詩人、實驗文本寫作者、Xi Nan & Fish Lu STUDIO, London 聯合獨立出版人。他也是本書作者西楠的人生伴侶，目前兩人生活在非洲。）

contents

目錄

Part One: The Answer | 第一輯: 回答

The Answer

The world is a
vast metaphor

I sit inside it
uncertain of
how to respond

24th.Jun.2017.   in Guangzhou

回答

世界是一個
巨大隱喻

我在其中
不知該
如何答題

2017.6.24.   於 廣州

Mental Hospital

In this mental hospital there are
an entire hospital of doctors and
the only patient
They wield all their magical powers, do everything
so that when she wakes up in the middle of the night
no longer sees shadows dancing

6th.Jul.2017.　　　in Guangzhou

精神病醫院

這家精神病醫院住著
一整個醫院的醫生和
唯一的病人
他們各顯神通，無所不用
為使她在夜裏醒來
不再看見影子跳舞

2017.7.6.　　　於 廣州

Fairy

He was traveling in Spain
He went to a supermarket to purchase items
Standing in front of the supermarket, he saw
on the ground
full of sewage and trash
And on this pile of sewage and trash
there sat a fairy-faced girl
with her legs bent
in her twenties
grimy
a crew cut, and she was
injecting drugs into herself
After the injection, a few seconds later
she suddenly looked ahead
and burst into hearty laughter
displaying extreme
happiness and purity
Don't know what her fantasy was?
he asked
For the rest of the day, he
felt very depressed
He said his existing worldview
could not explain
this fairy in the trash dump

14th.Nov.2014.   in London

3rd

仙女

他在西班牙旅遊
他去超市買東西
站在超市門口，他看見
一地污水
一地垃圾
在這一灘污水和垃圾上面
曲腿坐著
一個面若天仙的女孩
二十來歲
髒兮兮
理平頭，她在
給自己注射毒品
注射完成，幾秒之後
她突然目視前方
哈哈大笑起來
快樂至極
純淨至極
不知道她的幻想是什麼?
他問
接下來的一整天，他都
很沮喪
他說他已有的世界觀
無法解釋
這個垃圾堆裏的仙女

2014.11.14.　　　於 倫敦

Untitled

I long for darkness
just as much as
I long for light
I shall
forever struggling
on the road leads from
sin to holiness

One poet says:
Someone has achieved
eternal fame
so farewell—
you follow your path, I'll follow mine

I'm no saint
nor do I aspire to be
Heaven—how dull
I shall
forever struggling
on the road leads from
sin to holiness

3rd.Oct.2016.   in London

無題

我渴望黑暗
正如
我渴望光明
我將
永久掙扎在
從罪惡通往聖潔
的道路上

詩人說:
有人已經
邁入不朽
那麼拜拜
就此別過

我並非聖人
也不想當聖人
天堂，多麼無聊
我將
永久掙扎在
從罪惡通往聖潔
的道路上

2016.10.3.　　於 倫敦

Freedom

Watched two movies:
Taliban
drug lords
taught children to handle guns and drugs
made them play 'Russian Roulette'
with a revolver
until one blew himself up
the big guys then held a naked woman
laughed, revealing the blackish-yellow teeth

It is said that in 1974
when Marina Abramović
had a loaded pistol held
to her head by the audience
her heart was filled with fear

She understood something by then
something I never saw until today:
freedom without boundaries
named same as Satan

30th.May.2017.   in Shenzhen

自由

看了兩部電影
塔利班
大毒梟
教兒童持槍和吸毒
讓他們用左輪手槍
玩兒"俄羅斯輪盤賭"
直到一人把自己崩掉
大佬們就摟著裸女
笑露黑黃牙齒

據說在 1974 年
當瑪麗娜‧阿布拉莫維奇
被觀眾用上膛的手槍
抵住頭部
她的內心充滿恐懼

她當時明白了一件事
這件事我直到今天才看清：
沒有界限的自由
與撒旦同名

2017.5.30.　　於 深圳

The Truth

Dear,
a poet says:
'Must see the truth behind the many masks'
Ah yes
Truth—the only thing that
touches my heart in this world
Truth—endures, unaided by memory
as it withstands
the test of time
But I'm always confused by
the truth of things
What exactly is 'true'
and what isn't?
Maybe 'truth' is just a
pseudo-concept
and there is, no 'truth' in fact
I once burned myself for it
drained myself, and yet
in the constant flow
of time
I gained nothing, nothing at all

5th.Jan.2017.   in London

真實

親愛的，
詩人說：
 "要在重重面具下看到真"
是啊
真實，是這世間
唯一令我心動之物
真實，不需要記憶
因它經得起
時間沖刷
但我又時常為事物的
真實性，所困擾
究竟什麼是 "真實的"
什麼又不是？
也許 "真實" 只是一個
偽概念
 "真實"，是沒有的
我曾為它，燃燒自己
榨幹自己，然而
在時間一成不變的
流逝中
我一無所獲，兩手空空

2017.1.5. 於 倫敦

The Answer to the Riddle

In this world, truth is too often
unwanted
I've deceived myself repeatedly
amidst concealed darkness and secrets
hidden behind names and appearances

5th.May.2015. in London

謎底

在這世間，真實也常常
不合時宜
我總為事物看上去的樣子
那麼名不符實，而
一次次陷自己於不義

2015.5.5. 於 倫敦

If Free Will is Only an Illusion

then why are people different?
I asked God
At that moment by the river
a tiny ant
climbed up my white dress
I watched it for a while, asked it not to crawl into the dress
so it did not crawl into my dress
I said let's have some intimacy
so it crawled on my skin, lingering
I worried that I was too huge for it
and any movement would hurt it
I wanted to let it go
but it wasn't going the way I showed it
I also worried when my parents saw it when I got home
they would crush it
so I still wanted to let it go…
But at this moment
it'd crawled over my neck, crawled over my ear
and off to who knows where

Oh right, is this one the same little ant I saw last time?

5th.Jul.2017.   in Guangzhou

如果自由意志只是一種幻覺

那麼為何人與人各不相同？
我問上帝
這時河邊一隻
小螞蟻
爬上我的白裙子
我看了它一會兒，請它不要爬進裙子裡
它就不爬進裙子裡
我說我們發生親密關係吧
它就爬在我的肌膚上，纏綿悱惻
我擔心自己過於龐大
移動便會傷害它
我想放了它
然而它並不上我為它指的路
我又擔心回到家被父母看見
他們會摁死它
仍想放了它
然而這會兒
它爬過我的脖頸，爬過我的耳根
就不知跑到哪裡去了

噢對了，這和上次看見的小螞蟻是同一隻麼？

2017.7.5.　　　於 廣州

Prayer

'Fuck, what are you doing still?'
'Hurry up! Hurry hurry hurry up!'
'We need to pray'
'to eat breakfast'
'to change clothes'
'Need to go downstairs'
'Fuck! And we're late again'
'Hurry hurry hurry up!'
He very anxiously finished
a bunch of words, like
a machine gun firing, and then
closed his eyes, put his hands together, a pious
face in time
voice soft:
'Our Father in heaven'
'please bless our family'
'joy, harmony, sunshine'
'Pray in the name of Jesus'
'Amen!'

20th.Sep.2016.   in London

禱告

"他媽的，還在幹什麼咯？"
"快點！快快快！"
"還要禱告"
"還要吃早餐"
"還要換衣服"
"還要下樓"
"媽的！又遲到了"
"快快快！"
他火急火燎說完
一串話，像
機關槍掃射，之後
閉眼，雙手合十，及時地
換上一副虔誠面孔
嗓音柔和:
"我們在天上的父"
"請保佑我們全家"
"喜樂，祥和，陽光"
"奉主名禱告"
"阿們！"

2016.9.20. 於 倫敦

History

Less and less believe in our eyes
Histories
are written by humans, and how limited
our eyes are
And, gradually realizing that
numerous things in the world
can be attained through deceit
it deals a fatal blow to
the very essence of truth
However, Yu was quite confident:
'You're alive, people are alive
—this in itself shapes the course of history,'
He further said:
'The collective existence of every individual—
profoundly influences the course of history.'
He did say:
E—v—e—r—y individual
So, I am thinking, if
e—v—e—r—y individual
creates and destroys
within their own realm
in the confines of their personal space
objectively, this period of history
indeed exists
Therefore, a history does not
necessarily require any connection
with others
to be deemed as such, does it?

12th.Nov.2013.   in London

歷史

越來越不相信我們的眼睛
歷史
不過被人書寫，而我們的眼睛
多麼局限
並且，越來越感到
世間的許多事
通過欺騙便可獲得
這對真實，真是致命一擊
然而，Yu 信誓旦旦：
「你活著，人們活著
本身就在，改變歷史」
他還說：
「每一個人，活沒活過
都對歷史，造成很大影響」
他的確是說的：
每、一、個、人
我在想，如果
每、一、個、人
一間自己的房間
自行創造
自行毀滅
在客觀上，這段歷史
也確實存在過
所以，歷史，原來
不必非得和他人
發生什麼關係
才叫，歷史，麼？

2013.11.12.　　　於 倫敦

The Question of Predators' Innocence

Due to
hunting
attacks
on captive livestock, and
the fear of humans
wolves'
habitats are said to be
massively destroyed

1st.Jul.2013. in London

掠食者的清白問題

據說由於
對圈養牲畜的
獵捕
攻擊，以及
人類的恐懼
狼
的棲息地
被大量破壞

2013.7.1. 於 倫敦

Clams

We were sitting in an outdoor restaurant
by the river, eating
Italian seafood spaghetti
Y. picked up
a clam and said to me:
Marvel at this creature
its flesh, so tender
yet encased in
a shell, so tough

And I was thinking
it is being devoured by us
nonetheless

3rd.Jun.2013.　　　in London

蛤蜊

我們坐在河邊的
露天餐廳，吃
義大利海鮮面
小神仙挑起
一只蛤蜊，對我說：
你看它多牛哇
這麼軟的，肉
卻長出
這麼硬的，殼

而我在想
可它依然，正在
被我們吃

2013.6.3. 於 倫敦

Character

Can't pretend
who you are
You can only be
you, or
uprooted

22nd.Nov.2012.   in London

角色

無法假裝
你是誰
你只能是
你，或者
連根拔起

2012.11.22.   於 倫敦

On Subway

Play a game, sit in lines
Emoji: Be cold, be reserved
The spell coincides:
'We are all
blockhead
no talking
no laughing......'

Look: that defiant rule-breaker! Must be
drunks and lunatics!

—After unspoken sneers, on the subway
confident and content in our silent majority
we bask in our self-satisfaction

9th.Feb.2011.   in London

在地鐵

玩一個遊戲，排排坐
表情符號：要酷要淡定
咒語不謀而合：
　"我們都是
木頭人
不許說話
不許笑……"

瞧：那張狂的違規者！定是
醉漢與瘋子！

——腹誹之後，在地鐵上
因為人數優勢
我們沾沾自喜

2011.2.9. 於 倫敦

Two Chinese Writers

Discussing a book withdrawn from stores
due to political reasons
Writer A, born in the 1950s, said:
'This is a lesson from history
and we must exercise extreme caution
in our writing!'

In a private conversation following the meeting
Writer B and I, both born in the 1980s, revisited the topic
To my surprise, she blurted out:
'Senior Writer A indeed
served as our
wake-up call!'

Jun.2017.   on a highway in Guangdong

兩個中國作家

談及某部因政治原因
被下架的作品
50 後的 A 說:
這就是前車之鑒
我們下筆時要
謹慎, 再謹慎!

會後我和 B 又談及此事
B 和我同是 80 後
不料她脫口而出:
A 老師的確
為我們
敲響了警鐘啊!

2017.6.　　　於 廣東某高速公路上

Untitled

In August 2008, my ex and I
(that was the third year of our relationship)
were in the cheap council flat in East London
(less than 20 square meters)
sitting in the garish shabby sofa of our landlord's
On the opposite wooden table there was
the laptop that was falling apart
There were also two little fans whistling
under the laptop
(in case of overheating and a sudden shutdown at any time)
We opened our four eyes wide
staring at the screen with a lousy internet—
we were watching the Beijing Olympics
I remember clearly
when the five silvery-glinting rings
rose from the ground into the air
and some grand music played
I suddenly started to howl and cry
for some inexplicable reasons

18th.Apr.2018.   in Shenzhen

無題

2008 年 8 月我和前任
　(那是我們相戀第三年)
在東倫敦廉價出租屋
　(不足二十平米)
花裏胡哨的陳舊沙發上
對面木桌支一臺
快散架的手提電腦
電腦下還擺了兩扇
小風扇呼呼吹
　(以防隨時過熱關機)
我們瞪大四只眼睛
在卡得斷斷續續的網上
看北京奧運
我清楚記得
閃銀光的五環
從地面升上空中
宏大的音樂響起
這時
我突然莫名其妙地
嚎啕大哭起來

2018.4.18.　　於 深圳

In North X Village

1.
The old fans in the meeting room whirled
the leader of North X Village served the provincial leaders with
desserts made by the villagers, and then
he focused on the
export mountain spring from the village
Functions according to him:
a. laxative
b. loses weight
c. cures for baldness
d. anti-diabetes
blah—blah—blah...
On the white wall, the TV is singing:
'Red is the east
rises the sun
China has a Mao Zedong' (1)

2.
We followed the guide
looked at the bamboo woods, ancient houses, flowing stream
This mentally disordered
old woman in light-blue floral blouse
always followed closely behind, as if she
was one of us
She stood in the mud
jumping, singing, waving arms
and followed us to
get on our return bus
wouldn't get off anyway
until someone said:
This bus is going to Guangzhou

she suddenly changed her mind
slowly squeezed out of the bus door

9th.Jun.2017.　　　on a highway in Yangjiang, Guangdong

(1) "Red is the East" (or "The East is Red 東方紅") is a Chinese revolutionary song that was the *de facto* national anthem of the People's Republic of China during the Cultural Revolution in the 1960s.

在北 X 村

1.
會議室的老風扇呼呼轉
北 X 村領導給省領導端上
村民做的甜品，然後
他重點介紹本村
外銷山泉：
一能通便
二能減肥
三治禿頂
四防糖尿病
……
白牆上，電視裏在唱：
東方紅
太陽升
中國出了個毛澤東

2.
我們跟隨導遊
看竹林，古屋，流水
這個精神失常
穿淺藍花衣的老太
始終緊隨在後，好像她
本就是其中一員
她在泥地裏
跳躍，唱歌，揮舞手臂
又跟著我們
上了返程大巴
怎麼也不肯下去
直到有人說：
這輛車開往廣州
她突然改變主意
慢吞吞蹭出車門

2017.6.9. 於 廣東陽江某公路上

Listen

If I talk about death
don't panic
listen to death, like
listening to life, like
listening to ordinary sounds and
soft poem lines

Let us, put it straight—
the thing is
not very beautiful, but
never sadder
than surviving
in this world

28th.Jan.2011.   in London

聆聽

假如我談到死亡
勿需慌張
就像聆聽生活一樣，聆聽
死亡，像
聆聽聲音和
柔軟的詩章

還是，把話說白了吧
這件事它也
並不美，但
決不比活著
更悲傷

2011.1.28.　　　　於 倫敦

You Can't Say

When I truly fear to be
a slave to desires
there's no questioning my
deep reverence for reason

When I weary from the
monotony of obeying rules
you cannot mock my newborn heart—
untamed and fresh as a wild horse

16th.Jul.2012.　　in London

你不能說

當我真實地懼怕成為
欲望的奴隸
你不可置疑我
對於理性的崇高敬意

當我實在地厭倦跟從
規則的無趣
你不可譏諷我
一枚野馬般的赤心

2012.7.16.　　　於 倫敦

Part Two: My Sin | 第二輯 我的罪

The Body

This body in front of the full-length mirror—
color in sallow
shape in sagging
The bluish-grey bra straps are
stuck
in the skin
leaving deep-red sunken marks
but you remember, the past is like smoke
did not leave a trace
The curves
spreading from under the armpits to the sides of the bra
the ups and downs of the curves
are the accumulated fat
can't be carried by this narrow and small bra;
are the sin and beauty
laughs and cries
you've swallowed for all these years
Down the earlobes
across your gentle neck
wandering on your shoulders that are still flat
you feel a little more confident
as if your youth is still there
But further down, it's your arms
slightly clamping

there's an excess layer of waxy
flesh
that you're unfamiliar with
It's your lost rivers and mountains
leaving only a mess and emptiness
Click, you untie your bra
jumps out in the mirror: a pair of breasts
a pair of breasts
a pair of soldiers who are about to retire
middle-aged and getting fat
embarrassingly looking at each other
They are two cloudy pupils: open
look around
Now, you turn your body
facing the full-length mirror sideways
you see: a rising belly
your eighteen-year-old never returns
You look to: the growing belly
like it's preparing for, a baby who hasn't yet arrived
You hate this too-early preparation
you feel like a piece of
gift in a buy one get one free bundle
You feel confused
you still feel confused about many things
This year you are going to be thirty
The legs getting bigger under the belly
has stricken your fear
fortunately for the moment being
they are tightly wrapped in
a pair of jeans
there's still a safe distance
between you two
You just bare your upper body
like this

36th

The upper body
what on earth is the relationship
between the upper body, and the lower?
You just bare yourself like this
looking into the full-length mirror—
you look at me
tremble your lips
made no sound

4th.Jun.2015.　　　in London

身體

穿衣鏡前的這一具身體
色澤蠟黃
形態鬆弛
藍灰色內衣綁帶
勒
在皮膚裏
留下深紅凹陷的印記
你卻想起，往事如煙
並不著痕跡
從腋窩下蔓延至內衣側邊的
曲線
跌宕起伏的曲線
是窄小內衣無法承載的
囤積脂肪
是你這些年來吞咽下的
罪惡與美麗

歡笑與哭泣
耳垂向下
劃過你溫和的脖頸
漫步在你尚平坦的雙肩
你稍許自信
仿佛青春還在
但再往下，是你的手臂
輕夾緊
就多出一層：你所陌生的
蠟黃色的
肉
是你失掉的江山
空餘一片狼藉
啪嗒，你解開內衣
鏡中跳出：一對乳房
一對乳房
一對行將退役的士兵
中年發福
面面相覷
是兩只混濁的瞳孔：打開
張望
現在，你轉一轉身子
以側面朝向穿衣鏡
你看見：日益隆起的小腹
你的十八歲一去不返
你看向：日益隆起的小腹
像在給尚未到來的嬰孩，做準備
你厭惡這過早的未雨綢繆
你感到自己像件
買一送一的贈品
你感到困惑
你仍對很多事情感到困惑
這一年你將要奔赴三十
小腹下逐漸壯碩的雙腿

擊中你的恐懼
還好這會兒
它們緊包裹在
牛仔褲腿裏
你們之間尚有一段
安全距離
你就這樣裸露著
上半身
上半身
上半身，和下半身之間
究竟有著怎樣關係？
你就這樣裸露著
看向穿衣鏡裏
你看向我
顫動一下嘴唇
沒有發出聲音

2015.6.4. 於 倫敦

Female Bodies in Spa

In the Women's Section of a spa
I often witness
an array of bare bodies:
some full-figured
others slender
a few aged with wrinkles
and a handful young and firm
...
They don't resemble the enticing and sensual
figures portrayed in literature
nor do they invoke feelings of
shame or mystery in me

28th.May.2017.   in Shenzhen

水療館內的女體

水療館的女賓部內
我經常看見
一具具白花花的肉體：
肥頭大耳的
瘦骨嶙峋的
年老色衰的
青春跋扈的
……
她們既不像書裏說的
婀娜又美豔
也不讓我感到
羞恥或神秘

2017.5.28.   於 深圳

My Sin

You are endlessly praising, lost in mixed feelings
Holding your precious golden baby and
speaking high and mighty about the world
as if you've been renewed and filled with wisdom

'O, how cute!'
People join in praise
'O, how cute!'
I echo emptily

But the truth is, I'm overwhelmingly sad
'In the worst case scenario
women giving birth
is no different from pulling out a pumpkin of the body'

Yet society tells me,
'Childbirth is the
happiest thing in the world'
Something I can't quite grasp

Swollen, obese, warped beauty standards...
Hormone imbalances, mood swings...
And 'the continuation of life' —o, this biggest lie...
mothers are still facing death

And people are still living in this chaotic world
in a confused way—
it seems like a tragedy
why should we 'continue' anyway?

But in this moment

people are gathering around me
pointing fingers at my nose
'You woman with a womb but no child

you are sinned!'
Among the many faces appearing like ghosts
I recognize some familiar ones
some fellow townsmen and old friends, some casual acquaintances
(Casual acquaintances are always warmhearted on such matters)

People are gathering around me—
pointing fingers at my nose—
'You woman with a womb but no child
you are sinned!'

17th.Apr.2016.   in Guangzhou

我的罪

你們口吐蓮花，你們悲喜交加
你們懷抱著你們純金的嬰兒
發表對這世界的慷慨感言
仿佛大徹大悟

"呀，多麼可愛！"
人們交口稱讚
"呀，多麼可愛！"
我鸚鵡學舌

可我心情悲慟
"最壞的情況下
女人生育
無異於拉出了個南瓜"

社會又對我說：
"生育是這世上
最喜悅的事"
這話我也不明白

臃腫，肥胖，審美扭曲……
內分泌，荷爾蒙，性情古怪……
還有"生命的延續"——這最大的謊言呵……
我們仍然面對著死亡

人們仍然生活在混沌的世界當中
生活得如此不明就裏
這多像一個悲劇
何以還要"延續"？

然而此刻

人們聚攏過來，團繞在我身邊——
人們伸出食指，指點在我鼻尖——
"你這有著子宮而不去生育的女人

你是有罪的！"
在這幻影般浮現的無數面孔當中
我辨識出一些熟悉的臉
一些父老鄉親，一些點頭之交
（點頭之交在這類事情上總是古道熱腸）

人們聚攏過來，團繞在我身邊——
人們伸出食指，指點在我鼻尖——
"你這有著子宮而不去生育的女人
你是有罪的！"

2016.4.17.　　　　於 廣州

Women's Resentment

Onstage, the vocalist pours her soul into every note
Yet offstage, a murmur of critique begins
They regard the young performer, costumed and preened for the spectacle
Their gazes, steeped in bitterness
Older women sneer, their faces twisted in disdain
'Too skinny!'
'Where's her figure?'
'Just a country bumpkin!'
They pay no mind to her vocal prowess
ignoring the earnest effort of her performance

Then I comprehend
how a beauty
is slowly whittled to mediocrity
by the crowd's judgment
Or perhaps, simply led to her demise

'All the resentment women bear for each other,
is their disdain for prostitutes.' (1)

13th.May.2016. in Beijing

(1) The last sentence was inspired by Chinese writer Chen Xiwo (陳希我).

女人的仇恨

舞臺上的歌手縱情演唱
舞臺下的她們交頭接耳
面對一個盛裝出演的
年輕女孩，年老女人們
愈加地苛刻嚴厲
皺眉，鼻子嘴唇擠成了一團：
"太瘦！"
"沒腰！"
"不好看，小家子氣！"
沒有人評價她的唱功
也不關心演技

我於是明白了
美麗的女人
如何一步步在輿論中
走向平庸
或者死亡

"所有女人對女人的仇恨，都是女人對妓女的仇恨"(1)

2016.5.13.　於 北京

(1) 末句靈感來自中國作家陳希我。

Epitaph

Once more, as she had for three decades
a woman prepared breakfast for her husband and daughter
A smoked cigarette and a minor dispute
left her face drawn
her hands folded in prayer, pleading:
'Lord,
if our marriage
our family—is a mistake
please guide the weak'

She stayed faithful to her family, until her final breath

Then there was another woman, who was still young
about to greet her thirties
She had family, friends, a job, a lover
laughter and joy
growing uninhibited
like a fiery, thorny rose
Her vast postcard collection narrated tales of
Southampton's boats, Durham's castles
Singapore's night markets, Berlin's old watchtowers...
Antarctica awaited her

She was consistently faithful to herself
vowing to stay that way until her demise

Time's sharp claws crept over
their reluctant faces
their bodies that resisted to grow old
leaving scarlet trails
Both ultimately bid farewell to this world

in the same way

Yet, at the end
their lives were
undeniably so different

20th.Apr.2016.　　　　in Guangzhou

墓誌銘

三十年如一日，她再次
為丈夫和女兒做好早餐
因為女兒在早餐前吸掉的一支香煙
並且和丈夫發生了一點兒口角
她皺起眉頭，面容苦難
雙手合十，禱告：
　"主啊，
倘若我們的婚姻是一個錯誤
倘若我們的家庭是一個錯誤
請為軟弱的人指明道路吧"

她始終忠誠於家庭，直到死亡

而另一個人，她尚年輕
三十歲的幻影方才朝她招招手
她擁有親人，朋友，工作和情人
亦飲酒作樂，醉生夢死
自由生長
如同一株帶刺的火紅玫瑰

在她寄給自己的一大本明信片裏，躺著：
南安普頓的船隻，杜倫的城堡……
新加坡的夜市，和舊時的柏林崗哨……
她還將前往南極

她始終忠誠於自己
她想她將如此忠誠下去，直到死亡

歲月的尖利指甲爬過
她們的面容
她們不忍老去的身體
留下血紅的道印
她們終於告別這世界
並無二致

但畢竟
她和她
曾經大相徑庭地活著

2016.4.20.　　　　　於 廣州

Can't Get it Up

At the party
man A flashed a sly grin
hinting at a secret:
'You wouldn't believe it
but that night, they all paid for
a prostitute, and I didn't'
Man B quirked an eyebrow
joining in: 'Me neither
For some reason, just can't do it with strangers'
C, after a gulp of strong tea and a mouthful of leaves:
'Dull, really.
Can't even get it up'

5th.Aug.2017.   in Beijing

硬不起來

聚會上
男同學 A 面露狡點微笑
有點兒神秘：
　"你們不知道那晚"
　"他們都要了小姐，我沒要"
男同學 B 迅速一挑眉：
　"這事兒我也幹不來"
　"不知怎麼，不喜歡陌生人"
C 呷一口濃茶，啐出茶葉：
　"沒勁"
　"硬不起來"

2017.8.5.　　　於　北京

Outside the Bonds

After four years of marriage, she fell for another—
a writer
Soon, she was expecting his baby
He was quick to vow his determined bachelorhood
Defying the world, she bore the child
and vanished without a trace
The last time I saw her, I asked:
'How have you been, all these years?'
With a soft smile and eyes that danced:
'Look at me, what do you think?' she replied

7th.Aug.2017.   in Beijing

私生子

結婚四年，她在婚外
愛上一個男作家
不久懷孕了
男作家趕忙宣稱自己是
獨身主義者
她站在全世界的對面
生下這孩子
遠走高飛，不告而別
最後一次見她時，我動容：
"這些年，你過得好麼？"
她眼光波動，淡淡笑：
"你看我，過得還好嗎？"

2017.8.7.　　　於　北京

Sally

Leather bracelet: a fan of rock when you were young
Large man's watch: they almost destroyed your heart
Black nail polish: those never-abandoned rebellious thoughts
Someone interrupts your contemplation; they call for you:
Sally.
Sally, Sally,
were you always as tough as a stone?
Holding your breath, running along
eyes wide in the middle of the night
this is how I imagine you
When sit on a roller coaster I don't cry out
neither do I submit
I lift weights at gym with the mouth shut tight
training myself to mask emotions
Sally, your crow's feet have spread like weeds
how I wish I could smooth them away
I look at you and imagine myself ten years later
Some say, there is a reason to carry on

19th.Dec.2012.   in London

薩莉

皮制手鏈：迷醉搖滾的青春歲月
寬大男士手錶：他們險些毀掉的你的心
黑色指甲油：未曾打消的叛逃念頭
有人打斷你沉思，他們叫你：
薩莉
薩莉，薩莉
是否有個堅若磐石的過去
那些，女人摒住的呼吸，飛奔的腳步
深夜裏睜大的眼睛
這樣想像你
坐上過山車我從不吱哇亂叫
也不可一臉順服
緊閉雙唇我在健身房揮動啞鈴
鍛煉自己的面不改色
薩莉你眼角溝壑如雜草鋪陳
多想為你撫平
我看著你想像十年後的自己
人們說，活下去是有意義的

2012.12.19.　　　　於 倫敦

When I Think of Pain, I Think of My Belly

When I think of pain, I think of my belly
echoing: menstrual flow
such a feminine term it seeks
like seabirds, tides, the moonlight
Behind blackout curtains I peacefully sleep
for there are moments I desire no light at all
Three sleep masks in my possession
evidence of this recurring plight
One particular winter day
lay down with eyes open wide, from dawn to dusk
on a plush mattress, feeling adrift, as if in the middle of the ocean
England's winter light retreated prematurely
enveloping everything in a pure, uninterrupted black
In comparison, tears seem misplaced
Sometimes crowds walk in silence and I light a cigarette
the crowds are walking just like smoke rings curling up
During a power outage, I seated on the bathtub
a cigarette lit against the consuming darkness
That mix of silence, smoke, my confined space
I can't tell you how wonderful it was
Have you ever felt the allure of near suffocation?
The sensation of holding one's breath
and then the exhilarating release as if you were reborn
akin to the sharpness of tequila
or a sultry ballet on tiptoes
When the wind tangles my hair I sing a song with my face
impassive
Sunlight hits my eyes do you know how sorrowful I am
A damp underground inn, cockroaches, distant motors, young
hip-hoppers downstairs, violence, sex, drugs, a banker's wife, a
prime minister's wife, the great motherhood, love, prostitutes,

thieves, love, death, pistol, writing writing writing, love, death, love love love, death death death, a serene island rests upon an endless ocean
I pen aimless poems
as the grape tomatoes and smoked bacon I've just consumed

12th.Jul.2013.　　in London

一想到疼痛我就想起我的小腹

一想到疼痛我就想起我的小腹
比如：經血
多麼女性化的一個詞語
比如：海鳥，潮汐，月亮
諸如此類的一切
把遮光窗簾拉緊安穩地睡上一覺
有時我不需要光線
為此我甚至收藏了三件眼罩
某年冬天的一個日子
從清晨醒來睜眼躺到午後
滾動在巨大綿軟的床墊上好似在海中央
然後是英格蘭冬季早逝的光
純黑色，整日的純黑色
相形之下眼淚難以啟齒
有時人群在寂靜中行走我就點燃一支煙
人群行走的樣子就像煙圈裊裊上升
一次停電的時候我正坐在浴缸上抽煙
吮嚼一下的純黑色
還有寂靜，還有香煙，還有我的封閉的狹小的空間

我無法告訴你那有多美妙
你是否嘗到過窒息的滋味?
緊憋住一口氣許久
呼地一下放開你就以為你又活了一回
你就以為你又飲下一杯慘烈的龍舌蘭
你就以為你又旋轉腳尖跳出一支淫蕩的芭蕾
風兒把頭髮吹亂的時候我作出若無其事的表情歌唱
陽光從頭頂斜斜地鑽進眼睛裏你知道我多憂傷麼
潮濕的地下旅館，蟑螂，遠處的馬達聲，樓下的嘻哈青年，
暴力，性，毒品，銀行家的妻子，首相的妻子，偉大的母愛，
娼妓，小偷，愛，死亡，手槍，寫作寫作寫作，
愛，死亡，愛愛愛，死亡死亡死亡，
安全秀美的小島漂浮在無邊無際的大海上
讓我就這樣寫下一首沒有始終的詩
就像我剛剛吞下的小番茄和醃培根肉片

2013.7.12.　　　　於 倫敦

I Have a White Polyester

Strap-shoulder Nightdress

I have a white polyester strap-shoulder nightdress
and a beige trench coat with epaulettes
Every noon
I put on the nightdress, and the trench coat
go downstairs to the supermarket to buy food
The white male neighbor I encountered in the elevator, said:
'That's a really cool outfit!'
I like to
pass by the big glass door of the supermarket
and turn my head to look at my side figure inside:
upper body, with the straight trench coat on
next to the feet, the lace edge of the
white nightdress, lifted by the wind
lifted backwards, along with
the raised high-heels
making a beautiful arc
I can also hear the sound of the high heels
clatter
clatter
stepping on the bricked floor

18th.Aug.2013.   in London

我有一條白色滌綸吊帶睡袍

我有一條白色滌綸吊帶睡袍
還有一件帶肩章的米色風衣
每天中午
我穿著睡袍，披上風衣
去樓下超市，買食物
電梯裏碰見的白人鄰居，說：
"睡袍外面裹風衣，很酷啊！"
我喜歡
經過超市大玻璃門時
扭頭看裏面的側影：
上半身，風衣挺拔
腳旁，白色睡袍的
蕾絲邊，被風揚起
向後揚起，連著
抬起的高跟鞋
劃出漂亮的弧線
還能聽見高跟鞋
咯咯咯
咯咯咯
踩在鋪磚地面的聲音

2013.8.18.   於 倫敦

61st

Eyes

Can't forget those eyes
sizing up, staring...tightly nailing
Sometimes you laugh
Sometimes I scream
At these times I am a vessel
a blow-up doll, or
a lab rat
an anarchist in the concentration camp
Sometimes I probably have those same eyes
forced or innate
People affirm the necessity to 'observe'
slowly you get used to it

21st.Dec.2012.   in London

眼睛

忘不掉那些眼睛
打量，緊盯……緊釘
有時你們發笑
有時我尖叫
這些時候我是器皿
是充氣娃娃，或者
實驗室裏的小白鼠
集中營裏的無政府主義者
有時我大概也有這樣一雙眼睛
被迫或與生俱來
人們肯定"觀察"的必要性
慢慢你就習慣了

2012.12.21.　　於　倫敦

Redhead Woman in Council House

There is a council building
on my way to the supermarket
This afternoon
a redhead woman was
standing on the balcony of the second floor

A
redhead
woman

Red hair was made into an unkempt bun
Her black camisole tightly wrapped
the body in her thirties
Right hand holding a cigarette while waving
left hand grabbing a cellphone
And her mouth was
shouting into the phone
A quarrel between lovers
kept quarreling and domineering
She
looked
so sexy

She looked so sexy

So I took another look at the
dilapidated council house
behind her
that man like a wolf
who didn't show up
and all the emptiness

took place in that room

28th.Jun.2013.   in London

廉價公屋裏的紅髮女人

在我去超市的路上
有棟政府廉價公屋
今天下午
二樓陽臺站著
一個紅髮女人

一個
紅髮
女人

紅髮蓬亂地挽起
黑色吊帶背心緊裹
三十來歲的身體
右手夾香煙揮舞
左手抓手機
而她的嘴
正對著話筒叫嚷
情人間的爭吵
吵哇吵飛揚跋扈
那模樣
簡直
性感死了

那模樣簡直性感死了

我於是又看了一眼
她身後
那間破舊的公屋
那個沒露面的
狼一樣的男人
連同在那屋裏發生過的
一切虛無

2013.6.28.　　於 倫敦

Mother-to-be

She is becoming a mother
her belly round and full
a parabola outlined by
the horizontal stripes of her tight outfit
She sits as straight as possible
slightly raising her head
upturned mouth corners
a tall nose and, long eyelashes
In front of her there are
a milkshake
colorful fashion magazines
Outside the cafe
the sun's shining brightly
on the blonde lady
sitting opposite to her

How glad I am to see
a mother-to-be, with fashion magazines
placed in front of her
instead of
baby-care books
They two are chatting in high spirits
and she smoothly rolled her long hair
into a loose bun at the back of her head
obviously did not cut her hair
and try to
'make the baby more nutritious and healthy'
She's wearing beige cropped pants
beach flip flops
and a flashy
orange leathered handbag, tilted at her feet
As a mother-to-be
she doesn't have to
'end her old life
and start a new one', does she?
I go out for a cigarette
go around her
At this moment the Latin dance music
in the cafe is passionate as fire
the mother-to-be closes her eyes, indulges
shakes her body
together with, that parabola
—the dance of a young girl

8th.Aug.2012.   in London

准媽媽

她將成為一個媽媽
腹部渾圓飽滿
白底橫條的緊身衣下
繃出一條拋物線
儘量挺拔上身
微揚頭
嘴角上翹
高鼻樑與長睫毛
她的面前有
奶昔
時尚雜誌花花綠綠
咖啡館外
陽光璀璨
投向她對面
金髮小姐的身上
我多麼高興看見
一位准媽媽，面前擺放著
時尚雜誌
而不是
育嬰手冊
她倆神采飛揚聊天
她順手將長髮在腦後
挽成鬆散的髻
顯然並沒有剪髮
沒有企圖以此
"使嬰兒更營養健康"
她穿米黃色七分褲
夾趾沙灘涼拖
張揚的
橙黃皮包，斜靠腳邊
作為一位准媽媽

也不必非得
結束什麼舊生命
開始什麼新生命吧？
我出門抽煙
繞過她
這會兒咖啡館裏
拉丁舞曲似火
准媽媽閉上眼沉醉
扭呀扭
連同，那條拋物線
少女之舞

2012.8.8.　　　　　於 倫敦

Flamenco Dancer

A red Moon
A black Sun
A woman
with pain in her whole body
sinks back
Iron nails
pierce through her belly
Hanging in mid-air
with one leg being a pendulum:
Ta
Ta-da-da
Ta-da
Before death visits

she's in passionate love with illusions
indulging in the uncertainties
those unnamed
invisible things
Running towards, fleeing from, in such cycles
On a leaping bull's back
filled with spears, silence is a treasure
Her menstrual blood stains a flower
on the right ear, she then holds
her skull
to kiss
to revenge, before collapsing:
Ta
Ta-da-da
Ta-da
Ta
Ta-da-da
Ta-da
I know that even Christ's privilege
cannot halt
her pride

19th.Mar.2013.   in London

弗拉明戈舞者

紅月亮
黑太陽
一個周身疼痛的
女人

向後凹陷
從腹部穿過的
鐵釘
掛在半空，腿是鐘擺：
嗒
嗒嗒嗒
嗒嗒
死亡造訪以前
與幻象熱戀
沉溺於不確定
那些未命名的
隱形之物
奔向，逃離，如此往復
蹦跳的牛背上
插滿長槍，沉默是金
經血染紅右耳旁
一枚鮮花，然後提著
她的頭顱
去親吻
去復仇，坍塌以前：
嗒
嗒嗒嗒
嗒嗒
嗒
嗒嗒嗒
嗒嗒
我知道即使基督的特權也
沒法兒阻止
她的驕傲

2013.3.19.　　　　於 倫敦

Dad

You said on the phone
that you wanted to adopt a daughter
A muddled half-truth
When did I start using, smiles and indifference
as a facade?
Besides that time
after yelling at each other, you saw me off at the train
I hugged you
like a sweetheart from the previous life
tears old and worn
like a rusted knife
You struggled to stay in control
suspecting that I had defected
And I breathed in the mingled scents of the London Underground
replaying Chinese folk music
Headphones holding the music you wrote
notes evoking the past:
your youth, your glory years
the bright costumes you meticulously picked out for me
the standard hairstyle, and the nutritional recipes
You would roar when you punished me, and then secretly write in
your diary:
"Xi my child…
I'm so sorry…"
For poetry, you give me praise and criticism
experience has provided you with worldly wisdom
but you forgot that the traits of poetry and music
are like a genetic heritage
Open your eyes and take a look at the world. You said

You thought that I should live predictably and pragmatically
Sometimes you're more silent than usual
it makes me regret being born all the more
I guess it must have damaged your prestige
and aged mum
For many years, I turned from you two with flighted footsteps
yet at the same time I'd search the world for your shadow
I refuse to imagine that you'd die before me
or be shackled by illness
or that you'd lack happiness
but I often feel helpless
like I'm powerless against myself
like I feel powerless against everyone I've loved
I see stubbornness and suspicion in all
Could something as useless as poetry comfort you, Dad?
What about, moonlight as bright as the day?
After all, it is the same moon for you and me
I have dreamed of you and mum
walking on the riverside promenade, and in the woods
you walked by the nursery at the gate
not showing any emotion, turning right and walked into the world
And I am there
with a sad face, and a stubborn neck

Dad

I might never turn to religion
but I will pray for you often

8th.Feb.2013.   in London

爸爸

你在電話上說著
想領養一個女兒
真假摻拌
什麼時候起，微笑和漠然
成為我僅剩的華服
除了那一次
相互吼叫之後，你送我上火車
我擁抱你
恰似你的前世戀人
眼淚破舊
如腐鏽的刀
你難以自控
疑心我已叛逃
而我在氣味混雜的倫敦地下鐵
反復播放中國民族音樂
耳機裏是你譜的曲
音符喚起過往
你的青春，有過的光輝歲月
你曾一絲不苟為我指定鮮亮的服飾
標準髮型，和營養食譜
還有懲罰時的怒吼，又悄悄寫下日記：
"西兒……
我多麼抱歉……"
對於詩歌，你讚美而責備
經驗帶給你處世的智慧
卻忘了詩歌與音樂的共通性
像遺傳基因
睜開眼看世界吧。你說
你認為我該活得安穩實際

有時你比往常沉默
我便為自己的出生而難過
揣測它如何損壞了你的威望
使媽媽衰老
許多年了，我背向你們腳步如飛
一面在世間找尋你的影子
我拒絕想像你們早於我離世
或是為疾病所困
或不足夠快樂
可我時常感到無助
像對自己的無能為力
像我對愛過的每一個人感到無能為力
表像頑固而可疑
百無一用的文字能夠安慰你麼，爸爸
璀璨如同白晝的月光，能不能
那畢竟是同一枚月亮呵
我曾夢見過你們的樣子
行走在住宅社區的河邊，叢林
穿過大門口的幼稚園
不露聲色，右轉通往世界
而我正在其中
面目哀傷，脖頸倔強

爸爸

我也許永世不皈依宗教
卻將時常為你們禱告

2013.2.8.　於 倫敦

Part Three: You are Most like God
| 第三輯 你最像上帝

Temperament

You pass on your weight, your melancholy
directly to my core
I absorb them
into my veins
burying my rebellion and liberty
even deeper
morphing into, the person I've become
like the deep sea, so blue it's nearly black
in the darkness, roiling, swirling

'In your very temperament,
lies the paths you've traveled, the tales you've known
and the souls you've loved'

04th.Apr.2016.   in Beijing

氣質

你把你的沉重，你的陰鬱
傳遞給我
我把你的沉重，你的陰鬱
融入我的血液
將我的叛逆與任性
埋藏得更深
長成，這時的我
好似，藍得發黑的，海底
在暗處湧動，翻騰

"你如今的氣質裏
藏著你走過的路，讀過的書
你曾愛過的人"

2016.4.4.　　於 北京

Thorn

I think of you in the depths of night
sky is a piece of dark canvas
time is a shadowy vortex
The stark silence emphasizes my loneliness
as if there is a very delicate and sharp thorn
piercing in my heart
That thorn is you
With each breath, it stirs the pain
Removed, it leaves a small void

5th.Apr.2016.   in Beijing

刺

我在夜深人靜的晚上想起你
天空是一張漆黑的畫布
時間是一只漆黑的漩渦
出奇的寧靜強調了我的孤獨
仿佛有一根極細極尖的刺
紮在我的心臟
這根刺就是你
伴隨我的每一口呼吸，撩撥疼痛
拔出來，就留下一點空洞

2016.4.5.   於 北京

Lethargy

Since leaving you
I've been perpetually drowsy
Sleeping, now a refuge from the world
In my younger days
I'd escape with cigarettes, alcohol, and loud music
but time changes things
Cigarettes lost their allure
alcohol only deepens my sorrow
and loud music now pains my heart
Since parting with you
I'm constantly overwhelmed with lethargy
using sleep as an escape
Every day
I drift off, consumed by the despair of missing you
and quietly, almost imperceptibly, I awaken
only to plunge into a deeper, and deeper—desolation

5th.Apr.2016.   in Beijing

昏昏欲睡

離開你之後的日子
我總是昏昏欲睡
睡眠是逃避這世界的方式
在我更年輕的時候
也曾以香煙，酒精和吵鬧的音樂逃離
歲月流逝
香煙已不再如夢似幻
酒精更加速了我的心碎
吵鬧的音樂則令人心臟生疼
離開你之後的日子
我總是昏昏欲睡
睡眠是逃避這世界的方式
每一天
我在想念的絕望中不知不覺地睡去
又不知不覺，輕輕地醒來
在醒來的瞬間
陷入更深，更深的絕望

2016.4.5.　於 北京

Left Hand

At the bustling Piccadilly Circus
I weave through the crowd
one step closer, just to grasp
your left hand, unconsciously
offered to me as you move ahead
fearing if it slips away
it's gone forever

18th.Jun.2013.   in London

左手

在嘈雜的皮卡迪利廣場
我穿越攢動的人頭
跟緊一步，只為
握住你前行中不經意
伸向我的，左手
唯恐失散便是
永遠

2013.6.18.   於 倫敦

Wake Up and Farewell

Another sunny and bright afternoon, the summer is not far
I wake up

Recall once more, this is the real farewell
last summer—those unrestrained bursts of loud cries and laughs
let go. Quietly flowing through my body
like being swept by a tornado
rippling away towards the opposite direction and disappearing

My smooth leg fell asleep
and will never wake up again, I know
You held my face under the moonlight
the moment my tears turned into pearls, my rebirth was announced

So, fuck the miniskirts
even wearing black nail polish, I miraculously regain my virginity
like a young girl

Let me talk to you in the softest voice
if without tenderness, how can we go on?
Please you also take me with you. Take me with you as you escape
from this world
I thrive just amid your gentle and elegant ten fingers
when you clench, I obediently fall asleep
and when you open, I dance the most seductive dance for you only

Later I start to sit among the crowds and listen to other people's
stories
listen to the stories
write about the stories

and then tell the stories to many other irrelevant people
this is also a very happy thing

Besides you, this is the second thing that makes me happy
That's it. I am very satisfied

Another sunny and bright afternoon, the summer is not far
I wake up

The soul in the flame dies with its form
In the sea's embrace, I stand in your palm with thrill
dancing my most seductive dance for you only

Apr.2007.   in London

醒與告別

又一個陽光明媚的午後，夏天不遠
我醒了

再做一次回憶，這是真正的告別
去年夏天——那時候肆無忌憚的高聲哭笑
去吧．靜靜流過我的身體
像被一陣龍捲風席捲
朝著反方向再不見蹤影的蕩漾開

光潔的小腿睡著了
再不會醒來，我知道
你把我的臉在月光中捧起
淚水化為珍珠的瞬間，我的重生得以宣佈

那麼去他的超短裙吧
即使塗著黑色指甲油，我也奇跡般地重獲少女貞操

讓我用最溫柔的聲音和你說話
如果沒有柔情，我們又怎麼可能活下去？
你也要帶我離開。就像自己離開一樣的帶我離開
我就長在你溫文儒雅的十指之間
握緊的時候，我乖乖睡去
張開的時候，我把最風騷的豔情舞跳給你一個人看

後來我開始坐在眾人之間聽別人的故事
聽故事
寫故事
然後把故事告訴許多不相干的其他人
這樣也很快樂

除你之外，這是第二件讓我快樂的事情
這樣就可以了。我很滿足

又一個陽光明媚的午後，夏天不遠
我醒了

火焰中的靈魂隨同身體一起死去
海水中的我興奮不已蠱立在你的手心
我把最風騷的豔情舞跳給你一個人看

2007.4. 於 倫敦

A Thousand Years of Grace

Sailing a boat
you and I were going to a distant island

During the journey
I threw away my skirt, nail polish
threw away my perfume, and expensive cosmetics
You abandoned your wallet
and smashed your computer and sportscar to smithereens
with a high voice in anger, shouted at them:

Devils!

Trekking over mountains and waters
we traveled through time, through
hatred, greed and parting,
When reaching that green field
you came close to me, embraced me

Two noses rubbing against each other
Two bellies magnetically joined
Two arms entwined

We sowed twenty toes into the field
We grew into a tree
a thousand years of grace

(time unknown, in Newcastle, England)

美麗千年

駕一葉扁舟
你和我要去往遙遠的孤島

旅途中
我扔掉超短裙、指甲油
扔掉香水，和昂貴的化妝品
你把錢包丟棄
又將電腦和跑車砸得稀巴爛
怒目圓睜，高昂著聲音沖它們叫喊——

惡魔!

跋山涉水
我們穿越時光，穿越了
憎恨、貪婪與離別
到達那片碧綠田野之時
你走近我，擁抱我

兩只鼻子相互摩挲
兩片小腹吸磁般接合
兩雙手臂絞纏

我們將二十顆腳趾播種進田野
我們長成了一棵樹
美麗千年

(時間不詳，英國，紐卡斯爾)

Who to Save

Someone posted a question
on social media:
If my body and
soul
both fell into water
who would you save first?
So I went to ask Yu
'Your soul'
he replied

21st.Jan.2017.   in London

救誰

有人在社交媒體
發出問題：
我的身體，和
靈魂
同時掉進水裏
你先救誰？
我就去問小神仙
"你的靈魂"
他回答我

2017.1.21.   於 倫敦

Waiting for the Rain to Stop

It feels like forever since I ran through a wilderness
since I stood by the sea and cried
It's been too long since I kissed fearlessly
since I've truly embraced someone
I can't remember the last time I laughed and screamed while
crossing at a red light
or the last time I stayed up all night, watching the sunrise with
smudged makeup

There's so much more I haven't done in such a long time

Ichigo said:
When the rain ceases, go and run in the wilderness.

And Ichigo added:
May you feel embraced.

(time and place unknown)

等雨停

很久沒有在曠野中奔跑了
很久沒有面朝大海，痛哭一場了
很久沒有肆無忌憚地親吻了
很久沒有再和一個人裸身擁抱了
很久沒有在紅燈時笑叫著穿馬路了
很久沒有通宵達旦，再頂著殘妝等日出了

還有很多，很久沒有再做的事

一果說：
去啊，等雨停了，就去曠野中奔跑

一果又說：
願你感覺擁抱

(時間、地點不詳)

That Year

The body you'd fallen in love with
withered instantly
at the first stop of our escape

Wrinkles envelop
distorted promises, are the broken
songs you hummed that year

16th.Jul.2010.   in London

那年

你戀過的身體，在我們
逃亡的第一站
瞬間枯槁

皺紋裏夾
失真的諾言，是那年
你曾哼唱過的殘斷歌謠

2010.7.16.   於 倫敦

A Vast Wasteland

Minutes before dawn
you arrived unexpectedly
loved intensely just for a brief moment, then
minutes later
departed just as suddenly

Where you passionately loved and abandoned
stood a vulgar stone bridge, where
the air was cold enough to make one shiver
streetlights faintly warmed the air, leaving
our kisses damp

And before the wind could dry my lips
I quickly looked away, feigning
indifference
You acted as though
the sky was falling down
jumping around, grabbing my shoulder
then dawn broke
and like the wind, you vanished

With emotions still surging
a vast wasteland
grew in my chest
In the following seconds
I sat up in bed
making that same
indifferent expression

12th.Sep.2010.   in London

一片巨大的荒原

在天亮之前的十幾分鐘
你無預兆地來了
拼命地愛了一會兒，就為了
十幾分鐘之後
又毫無預兆地離棄

在你發瘋一樣狠狠地愛了又離棄之處
有一座俗裏俗氣的石橋，那裏
空氣冷得出虛汗
路燈曖昧地呵氣，弄得
那些吻也潮乎乎的

我未來得及被風吹幹嘴唇，就忙著
把眼睛斜向別處，做出
滿不在乎的表情
你還是一副
天要塌下來的樣子
上躥下跳，扳住我的肩
然後天亮了
你，風一樣絕塵而去

因為餘興未盡
我的胸口長出
一片巨大的荒原
接下來的幾秒鐘
我從床上坐了起來
做出
滿不在乎的表情

2010.9.12.　　於 倫敦

A Round Thing

After withered, tears
died in my belly

It once existed in my perception
but disappeared later without a trace
Then
my belly calmed

The smell of blood
mixed with the smell of excrement
and the smell of vomit
So
I lost its smell

What I remember about it
was a round thing
Just
a round thing

(time and location unrecorded)

一團圓

眼淚乾涸後
死在小腹裏

它曾存在於我的知覺中
卻又消失得無影無蹤
然後
小腹平靜了

血腥的味道
混雜著排泄物的味道
還有嘔吐的味道
於是
我遺失了它的味道

我所記得的它
是一團圓
僅是
一團圓

(時間、地點不詳)

HZ, it is not that I don't love you

I'm air, I'm transparent, my pain is a snake,
curls up in my body. I float upwards, and upwards, see the color of death,
that is an ocean of late autumn, deep yellow, roaring.

HZ, it's not that I don't love you.
You are my dreamland, you are my wasteland, you are a pond of blue water,
you are an illusion; you are a bubble, you are the pink sunset,
you are a ray of white spreads on the ground from the moonlight; you are also chains,
you are also walls, you are the sky that I cannot see the edge of.

Please do not look back when you leave, let us each suffer and almost die.
Let us die... Let us die... those sinful shells are staggering,
the fire of desire's going out. Flake out by the collapsed castle,
let us strive to open our eyes, and take another look at the flocks of birds slowly flying across the sky;
let us struggle to open our dry mouths, and taste the foul smell of rottenness once more.
And then—and then, all that remains is silence...

Can I be quiet now? Can I stop talking nonsense now?
Please do not caress my naked body;
I won't tremble because of thrill anymore.

(time unrecorded, in London)

HZ，我並非不愛你

我是空氣，我是透明的，我的疼痛是一條蛇，
蜷縮在身體裏。我往上飄啊飄，看見死亡的顏色，
那是一片深秋的海，深黃色的，咆哮著。

HZ，我並非不愛你。
你是我的夢境，你是我的荒原，你是一潭碧水，
你是一場幻覺；你是泡沫，你是粉紅夕陽，
你是月光灑在地上的一縷白；你也是鎖鏈，
你亦是城牆，你是我一眼望也望不到邊際的天空。

走的時候請不要回頭，就讓我們各自痛苦得幾乎死去。
死去吧，死去吧，那些罪惡的軀殼已經步履蹣跚，
欲望之火危在旦夕。就癱倒在那坍塌的城堡邊上，
讓我們吃力地睜開眼睛，再看一眼天空緩慢飛過的鳥群；
讓我們掙扎著張開乾涸的嘴，再一次品嘗腐爛的腥臭味兒。
然後——然後，一切便只剩下了寂靜……

現在我可以安靜了麼？現在我可以不再胡言亂語了麼？
請不要撫摸我光潔的身體，
我已不會再為之興奮地顫抖。

(時間不詳. 於 倫敦)

Some Words I Rarely Say

Some words I rarely say
neither coax from others
Such as:
"I love you," "I'll go this way," "Let's just—
drop it."
Instead
we drink and celebrate
gaze intently as we spin
Or head to the countryside
to the ocean
in our travels, we share profound
silence, looking back
silently marking
this unique moment that would never come back
There are words I rarely say
much like my inherent kindness and vulnerability
unwilling to bind
us
to a post destined for fire

(time and place unrecorded)

有些話我很少說出口

有些話我很少說出口
也不善誘他人說出口
比如:
我愛你;我走這邊;那就
算了吧
取而代之
我們飲酒作樂
在旋轉時伺機凝視
或者,去鄉村
去大海
旅途中別有深意地
沉默,回望
無言記住
這永不再來的一刻
有些話我極少說出口
如同我的仁慈與軟弱
不忍親手將
我們
系上火刑柱

(時間、地點不詳)

I Tried to Focus

I tried to focus
on washing the coffee stains in my cup
waiting for a kettle of water to boil
carefully
taking out the whole milk from the fridge
and the ground coffee
from the cupboard
I tried to focus
on these simple things, but I
ended up
staring at the ivory carpet
in the middle of the lounge
and—thinking of you

(time and place unrecorded)

我嘗試專注

我嘗試專注
專注於
洗刷杯中的咖啡漬
等待一壺水沸騰
認認真真
從冰箱取出全脂牛奶
還有櫥櫃裏的
咖啡粉
我嘗試專注
這些簡單的事物，卻以
緊盯客廳中央的
乳白色地毯
——想起你
而結束

(時間、地點不詳)

You Ask Why I Want to Meet You

You ask why I want to meet you
I say, just want to
see you, to see you
to touch you
to know you're alive
and true
and you're
smiling at me

(time and place unrecorded)

你問我為什麼想見到你

你問我為什麼想見到你
我說，就想
看見你，看見你
碰碰你
看見你，是活的
還會
對我笑

(時間、地點不詳)

Part Four: Your Loneliness | 第四輯 你的寂寞

Mama's Loneliness

'If you go on like this, you will end up miserable!'
'What evil did I do, to have given birth to you—such an unfilial daughter!'
'Go fool around with your pals! Don't ever call me mother again!'
I put on invisible earbuds
strode out of the house
wandered out all day long
When returning
you were wearing a light-blue gird apron
making dinner for me in the kitchen
face gloomy, like the sky about to rain
The kitchen smelled of oily fume that was
flavored of life
That's your smell
mama
your—smell of loneliness
There were other times
when I returned
you bent your back and sat on the sofa in the lounge
phoning your friends, to get some comfort
Your face was gloomy all the same
but you were faking some giggles
like you always taught me:
'Bring a smile in front of people'

'Don't wash your dirty linen in public'
Frankly speaking, mama
I hate your hypocrisy sometimes
Can I call it hypocrisy?
But now
you're still faking giggles
turning your cheeks to face the window
The setting sun throws in a ray of dull light
the light shines on your side face
and you are still so beautiful, mama
You always complain that I'm not as good at skin-care as you are
But, this beautiful side face
let me see again, in an instant, your loneliness
The side face in this dull light
that is your color—dull
Even when we were relatively calm
I was still willing to spend time outside
I was worried that once we were relaxed
it would detonate a bomb hidden who knows where
I went out, said goodbye to you
You were staring at the TV
with a hot-water-bag on your shoulder and neck
also said to me, goodbye
In the TV series on the screen there was
the dialogue between the 'Communist Army' and the 'Nationalist
Party'
battling wits and bravery
—every day entangled in such similar plots
That is your sound
mama
your—sound of loneliness
There were very few times
we sat quietly and ate together
Because of the love and fear to each other

we had no choice but to kept our mouths shut
and on the table left only
the sound of chewing
and the crackling typing sound when you
checked your cellphone from time to time
Was that a way for you to avoid embarrassment?
A very difficult meal
after the meal, we were both relieved
You went to the balcony and looked into the distance, stretching
don't know what was thinking in your head
In the end you turned your back to me
put your hands on your slender waist
one leg bent softly
like a fairly charming middle-aged woman that
no one really cared about
I slowly stretched out my hand
wanted to touch this
very charming shape of yours
However, beside of loneliness
I only reached
an imperceptible sigh
Sometimes, I hope you could
be happier, I hope you could
be lively, but
loneliness has overgrown in your body
Since my birth
you have grown into this
beautiful, lonely, woman
And that is why
mama
I don't want to have a child of my own

13th.Apr.2016.   in Guangzhou

媽媽的寂寞

"這樣下去，你不會有好結果！"
"我作了什麼孽，生出你這個不孝子！"
"去和你的朋友們鬼混吧！以後不要再叫我媽！"
我戴上隱形的耳塞
一個箭步沖出家門
整日在外遊蕩
返回時
你穿淺藍格子布圍裙
在廚房裏為我做晚餐
臉色陰沉，好像將落暴雨的天空
廚房裏飄出幾縷
充滿生活氣息的油煙味道
那就是你的味道
媽媽
你的，寂寞的味道
還有一些時候
當我返回時
你勾腰坐在客廳的沙發裏
給朋友們打電話，聊以安慰
你面色仍然陰沉
卻咯咯咯地假笑著
如同你教導我：
"在人前要面帶微笑"
"家醜不可外揚"
坦白說，媽媽
我有時厭惡你這樣虛偽
我可以稱之為虛偽嗎？
但這會兒

你仍在咯咯咯地假笑著
臉頰偏向窗外
夕陽投入一道暗啞的光
光線打在你的側臉上
你仍然那樣美麗，媽媽
你總是抱怨我不像你那樣善於保養
然而，這個美麗的側臉
讓我瞬間又窺見了，你的寂寞
暗啞光線下的側臉
那就是你的顏色，暗啞的
即使在我們相對平靜時
我仍樂於在外消磨時光
我擔心一旦鬆懈下來
就會引爆不知埋藏在哪兒的炸彈
我出門，和你說再見
你眼睛盯著電視
肩頸上放著熱敷袋子
也和我說，再見
電視劇裏傳來
共軍和國民黨鬥智鬥勇的對白
每天在大同小異的情節中糾纏
那就是你的聲音
媽媽
你的，寂寞的聲音
還有極少的時候
我們安靜地坐在一起吃飯
因為彼此相愛又懼怕
除了寡言，我們別無選擇
飯桌上只剩
嘰嘰呱呱咀嚼的聲音
和你不時抓起手機查看
劈啪的打字聲
那是你避免尷尬的一種方式吧
十足艱難的一頓飯

107th

飯畢，我們如釋重負
你走上陽臺遠眺，伸懶腰
頭腦中不知在想些什麼
最終你背對著我
將雙手叉在纖細的腰上
一條腿柔柔地打著彎
像一個味道十足
卻無人問津的少婦
我緩緩伸出手
想要觸摸你這個
無比迷人的形狀
然而，除了寂寞
卻只觸摸到
一聲不易察覺的歎息
時常地，我希望你能夠
更加快樂，我希望你能
熱鬧起來，可是
寂寞已經長在了你的身體裏
自我出生以來
你已然長成了這樣一個
美麗的，寂寞的，女人
這就是為什麼
媽媽
我不願有一個自己的孩子

2016.4.13.　　　　於 廣州

Some Love

You said, you rubbish
                What's the use for me to have given birth to you
You said, you idiot
                I'll sever the relationship with you
I don't want you anymore
I don't want you anymore
I don't want you anymore
                You said it three times in a row

Father phoned me
asked me to 'forgive you'
                'Even if the bones are broken, the tendons are still connected'
                He always thinks a family is, inseparable

It is not that, I can't forgive
but
some love, just
slowly fades away like this

5th.Jan.2017.   in London

有些感情

你說，你這個廢物
　　　　　我生下你有什麼用
你說，你這個畜生
　　　　　我要和你斷絕關係
我不要你了
我不要你了
我不要你了
　　　　　你一連說了三次

父親打電話給我
勸我 "諒解你"
　　　　　 "斬斷骨頭連著筋"

我並非，不能諒解，只是
有些感情，就是這樣
　　　　　漸漸流逝

2017.1.5. 於 倫敦

Harmony

Every Chinese New Year, she advises me
to phone and greet to all the relatives and friends
and gift 'lucky money' to the younger, elderly ones

Like on ordinary days, she tells me
'Family scandals should not go out of the house'
'Bring a smile in front of people'

She also loves to pour tea for everyone
at a dinner table
and so on

Throughout her life
my mother is pursuing a kind of
'harmony'
which I cannot accept
as it contradicts 'the truth'

1st.Feb.2017.   in London

其樂融融

過年了，她勸我
給所有親朋拜年
給小輩，晚輩打紅包

如同平日，她告誡我
"家醜不可外揚"
"人前面帶微笑"

她還熱衷在飯局上
給眾人倒茶
諸如此類

窮其一生
母親都在追求一種
我所不能接受的
與真實相抵的
"其樂融融"

2017.2.1. 於 倫敦

Mama, shut up!

Mama, you shut up!
My brain is about to explode
and I'm in a hurry
post office, supermarket, working overtime at night
Really Mama, you shut up!
What do you want what on earth do you want
Cursing like a machine gun doesn't help
I want to jump off the building if you continue
Every time hang up your phone
I really want to jump off a building
You always convince me that life sucks and I'm worthless
and forget about the urgent problems that must be solved
immediately
Oh, can we please get back to the real issue, Mama
Please get back to the real issue
Mama
You're not listening
The girl next to me slammed her phone
suddenly jumped up and spilled her coffee
before rushing out of that door
she presented her resentment
with her thoroughly deep love
but she awkwardly loves you, that mama

2nd.Feb.2012.   in London

媽媽別說了

媽媽別再說了
大腦就要爆炸
況且還趕時間
郵局，超市，晚間加班
真的媽媽，別再說了
您想怎樣您究竟想怎樣
機關槍一樣詛咒於事無補
再說我就去跳樓
每次掛上您電話
我真想跳樓
您總能叫我確信生活糟透了我一文不值
而忘記眼下亟待解決的問題
唉能回到正題上來嗎媽媽
請回到真正的問題上來
媽媽
您沒有在聽
鄰座女孩摔了電話
猛然跳起將咖啡弄灑
奪門而出前
以徹底的深情演繹了
怨憤
可她蹩腳地愛著您呢，那位媽媽

2012.2.2.　　於 倫敦

Not Giving In

Father
with one hand, he pointed
to the other
Strangely slackened
scattered with melting brown spots
abrupt and unclean
'They started appearing last year'
'One, two, three,'
'four, five…'
He counted to the tenth age spot
laughed drily:
'Damn, I'm not giving in'
'I still feel strong enough to pick a fight!'

26th.Jul.2016.   in Beijing

不服

父親
用一只手指著
他的另一只手
陌生的鬆弛上面
融化了零星的褐色斑點
突兀而不潔
"去年開始長起來的"
"一、二、三"
"四、五……"
他數到第十顆老年斑
乾笑一聲:
"媽的,老子不服嘞"
"老子精力旺盛得,直想找人打一架!"

2016.7.26.　　　　於 北京

Bonsai Kitten

Mama
you should strangle me
before I came to this world
otherwise
Papa would still destroy me
like what he's doing right now
I heard that
to squeeze a kitten into a
square jar
and given it enough time
its bones will be molded into
the shape of the jar
turning into
a square cat
very ornamental
However, I can't
and this has really disappointed you two
I'm fat like a pig
and mentally handicapped
In order to continue annoying each other
to pass your retired days
I have to shake my head
drooling
on my last legs

4th.Feb.2018.   in Guangzhou

正方形的貓

媽媽
你應當掐死我
在我來到這個世界以前
否則
爸爸也會幹掉我
像他正在做的那樣
我聽說
將幼貓塞進一只
正方形玻璃樽
日積月累
它就會和玻璃樽
長為一體
變成一只
正方形的貓
極具觀賞性
然而我不能
這真讓你們失望
我肥得像只豬
並且是個弱智
為了彼此繼續作對
以打發你們
退休後的時光
我必須晃著腦袋
淌著口水
苟延殘喘

2018.2.4.　　　於 廣州

Part Five: Solitude | 第五輯 孤獨

Untitled

Do you love me?
Let us dance

(time and place unrecorded)

無題

你們愛我嗎
我們跳舞吧

(時間、地點不詳)

June, London, a Kind of Comfort under the Sky

White cotton candies
grow on
a blue horizon
Floating seeds within
are solitary islands of freedom

Turning away from the world
the sun burns my right cheek
I lie back
on the vast green
imagining death is coming

1st.Jun.2013.   in London

六月，倫敦，天空下的一種安慰

白的棉花糖
生長在
藍的海平面
當中散開的飛絮
是孤零自由的島嶼

轉過頭，不看塵世
陽光曬得右臉頰發燙
我仰面躺在
廣闊的綠草之上
幻想永逝將至

2013.6.1. 於 倫敦

Days

Often at this time of a day
we've got nothing to do
we shout to each other
in the online instant chat group

'What are you doing?'
'So sleepy, waiting to get off work'
'Eating fruit, from morning to night'
'Drinking, messing around'
'Have been trying to read the "preface" of a book, but in fact in a
daze'
...

And then
the sleepy one continues to sleep
the drinking one continues to drink
the one playing on the cellphone continues to play on the cellphone

One day passes again

'Slow, is a speed of erosion'

17th.Jul.2015.   in London

日子

每到這個時候
我們無事可做
我們在聊天群裏
相互喊喊話

"你在做什麼？"
"好困，等下班"
"吃水果，從早吃到晚"
"喝酒，瞎混"
"始終在看'前言'，其實在發呆"
······

然後
好困的繼續睡覺
喝酒的繼續喝酒
玩手機的繼續玩手機

一天再次過去

"慢慢，是一種腐蝕的速度"

2015.7.17. 於 倫敦

Later, They Stopped Asking Me out for Drinks

Later
my habits changed:
I'd be home by midnight, then sleep
After that,
they no longer called me out for drinks
I wonder
if it was related to the midnight curfew
The last time we confided
they chattered:
Remember back then when you were also a sweetheart?
Remember in those days when you were wild too?
Speaking of these now
it feels like a past life

Later
they stopped asking me out for drinks

12th.Sep.2016.   in Beijing

後來，他們不再喊我喝酒

後來
我外出的習慣就變了：
在 12 點前到家，睡覺
後來
他們就不再喊我喝酒
不知道
和 12 點的門禁有沒有關係
最後一次吐露心聲時
他們七嘴八舌：
想當年你也是個妞兒啊
想當年你可有點兒瘋狂
現在說來
像是上輩子的事情

後來
他們就不再喊我喝酒

2016.9.12.　　　　於 北京

Paris in July · Good Old Days

On the streets of Paris in July
the city is a giant furnace
Some desires are burnt during the day
and rekindled from ashes at night
It takes me back to the summer of 2005
in Beijing
Just like you
I once savoured every desire
Then and now
always standing on
an open balcony jutting out to the street
consuming cigarette butts with our friends
then tossing them into the scorching air
imagining we were nimble tropical fish

8th.Jul.2015   in Paris

七月巴黎・大好時光

七月巴黎街頭
城市是一只巨大火爐
一些欲望在白天被燒毀
又在夜晚死灰復燃
這使我想起 2005 年夏天的
北京
我和你一樣
也曾嘗試體會每一種欲望
此時和彼時
總是站在
一截伸向街道的露天陽臺上
和夥伴們消耗一支支煙蒂
再把它們拋入炎熱的空氣裏
想像我們是靈巧穿梭的熱帶魚

2015.7.8.　於　巴黎

Long Ago

Long ago
we sat in Surbiton on New Year's midnight
discussing death
suicide, good and evil, and those lost to addiction
We talked about how to change this world
and surely the demons within everyone's heart
No doubt we had discussed many others
No doubt we had such conversations many times
in different places at different times
like in Brighton
or beside Canary Wharf, that Spanish restaurant
Long, long ago
in Surbiton, on New Year's eve
we spoke of death
Nearby, a river flowed quietly
and someone sang
'Auld Lang Syne'

31st.Jul.2016.   on a high-speed train from Beijing to Shenzhen

很久以前

很久以前
我們在新年午夜的索比頓
談論死亡
談論自殺，善惡，和吸毒者
我們談論如何改變這世界
甚至談論了
每個人心中的魔鬼
必定還談論過許多其他
必定還在不同時間的不同場所進行過
許多次這樣的交談
比如在布萊頓
在金絲雀碼頭旁的西班牙餐廳
很久，很久以前
我們在新年午夜的索比頓
談論死亡
不遠處有河靜靜流過
不遠處有人在唱
"友誼地久天長"

2016.7.31.　　　　於北京開往深圳的高鐵上

Youth

It surprises me—how long ago it was
and I still haven't forgotten: Autumn, 2003, G
was drenched in the rain, listening to a London lad busking
Scarborough Fair, his tears poured down
Summer, the same year, M sat
opposite a giant poster on Orchard Road, yelled to me
— 'Woman, I–wanna–get–laid!'
That summer, in a pub called 'Pink Angel'
we accepted men's perfumes and
roses, messily dancing
You said you loved watching me take off the shoes and jump on
the sofa
You said I was lazy and proud as a cat with a cigarette between my
fingers
How long ago it was, and I still haven't forgotten:
Summer, 2005, my long hair
dyed very red, the 'Ladies' Street' (女人街) that
hadn't yet been demolished, the 'Fairy Bar' (仙吧) where
we often ran into celebrities at late night. Notorious stars, by then
we were cleaner than they were, even though B
sought and failed every night for a one-night stand, Z
drunkenly and crazily danced, entertained the crowd
We kneaded some chewed gum, to cover
the license plate on a car, roared along, as if
death itself
How long ago it was, and I still haven't forgotten
this surprises me; river water flowing upstream
shattered pieces coming back together, and my time
reverses because of you all; how long ago it was
that was the youth I had lost:
the air conditioner that was constantly leaking in Singapore

130th

the scorching–sun–melted tarmac streets in Beijing
the ever–grey sky in Newcastle, England
...
'To know someone, you have to know what he (she)
was like in his/her twenties'

20th.May.2016.   in Beijing

青春

如此久遠，我仍然沒有忘記
這令人吃驚：2003 年秋天，G
淋成落湯雞，聽一倫敦小夥兒賣唱
《斯卡布羅市集》，淚如雨下
同年夏天，M 在
烏節路巨幅海報對面，沖我嚷嚷
—— 女人，我、要、豔、遇
這年夏天，我們在
名叫"粉紅天使"的酒吧裏，接受
男人們的香水和玫瑰，舞步淩亂
你說你愛看我脫下鞋跳上沙發的樣子
你說我一手夾煙慵懶又驕傲得像一只貓
如此久遠，我仍然沒有忘記：
2005 年夏天，染成
正紅色的長髮，那時還沒有拆除的
女人街，經常會夜遇明星的
"仙吧"，聲名狼藉的明星，那時
我們比他們更乾淨，儘管 B
每晚都想一夜情而未遂，Z

酒後狂舞，逗樂眾人
我們拉扯嚼過的口香糖，蓋住
車牌號，一路狂飆，仿佛
死亡本身
如此久遠，我仍然沒有忘記
這令人吃驚，河裏的水逆流而上
一地碎片重新凝結，我的時光
因你們而倒流，如此久遠
那是我走失的青春：
新加坡永遠在滴水的空調
北京被烈日曬化的柏油路
紐卡斯爾一片灰色的天空
......
"想瞭解一個人，便要知道他
二十歲時候的樣子"

2016.5.20.　　　　於 北京

One-way Ticket

Watching a teenage girl's dance class
from the upstairs of a gym
She
wore a high bun
dressed in, a plain black gymnastics outfit
Her limbs bared
'Swish—'
the smooth, slender legs, stretched
splitting, on the wooden floor of the basketball court
as a clean, beautiful straight line...
So I felt as regaining
that lost
smell, temperature, and time...
So I, for a moment, sank in a trance:
upstairs, downstairs
the teenager, and me
—is this teenager, me?

14th.Jul.2015.   in London

單程票

從體育館樓上俯瞰
一個少女的舞蹈課
她
挽起很高的髻
身著，純黑色體操服
四肢裸露
"唰——"
光潔細長的雙腿，繃直
在籃球場的木地板上，劈開
乾淨，漂亮的"一"字形
我於是仿佛重拾
那遺失的
氣味，溫度，和時光
……
我於是，霎那恍惚
樓上，樓下
少女，和我
這少女，是不是我？

2015.7.14.　　　　於 倫敦

Beijing Lyrics

O, I do love Beijing!
Especially now, at its dusk
Once in Beijing
my depression lifted
(leaving only the manic part)
My phone warns today
the air quality harms health
Yet, the smog and mask
fill me with fervour
The relapse of bronchitis
feels like a climax

28th.Mar.2018.   in Beijing

北京抒情

我真愛北京
這會兒可是
北京的黃昏呀
一到北京
憂鬱症全好了
　（只剩下躁狂的部分）
手機顯示今日
空氣質量危害健康
連霧霾和口罩都讓我
無比激動
氣管炎的發作好比
將事情推向了高潮

2018.3.28.　於　北京

Stereotype

Is a cripple surely kind-hearted?
Does an obesity surely have an outstanding soul?
Also:
should the blind, deaf, Quasimodo...
have no desire and be strong in spirit and noble and lofty and
perfecting themselves...every day?

If you run into a cripple
who curses you to die early
I mean—if

I'm going to stretch my heart a little bigger
until it can hold
the shadows and dirt of this world

22nd.Dec.2017.   in Guangzhou

刻板印象

跛子一定心地善良嗎?
胖子一定靈魂美妙嗎?
還有:
瞎子，聾子，卡西莫多……
是否就該無欲無求身殘志堅陽春白雪天天向上?

如果你碰見一個跛子
詛咒你早死
我是說——如果

我要把心臟再撐大一點兒
直到它能容納
世界的陰影和污垢

2017.12.22.　　於　廣州

Filling II.

The pain of life is inherent in life itself

I'm sitting by a horizontal striped wooden table
waiting for a panini, a cup of hot latte
Now
there should be an incoming call
a text message
or a conversation
of any kind
to make me think that some faking 'true–feelings'
do exist
I feel that hole again
that downwards swirling
cone-shaped, dark and narrow
empty hole
It grows right in the middle of my heart
At this moment I need a conversation
or some form of external aid
like needing to breathe
—a futile attempt to fill the hole

1st.Dec.2017.   in Shenzhen

填補 II

生命的痛苦孕育在生命本身之中

我坐在橫條紋木頭桌旁
等待一份意式帕尼尼，一杯熱拿鐵
此時
應當有一個電話進來
一條短信
或是隨便什麼形式的
一番交談
使我以為一些虛假的真情
確實存在
我又感覺到了那個洞
那個朝下漩渦的
錐狀的，又黑又狹窄的
空洞
它就生長在我心臟的正中央
此時我需要交談
或是什麼形式的外援
如同需要呼吸
徒勞地填補

2017.12.1.　　　　　　於 深圳

Mirror

I'm acrid and harsh
inventing issues where none exist
I charge forward without regard
seeing no one else in my way

I hide behind a righteous facade
saying one thing, doing another
My smile conceals a hidden knife
and I wear openly my shamelessness

I'm indifferent like salting a wound
I disdain like a silver needle piercing skin
I'm furious like a typhoon sweeping
I attack like a mad beast

'Why do you hurt me like this...'
—You appear so vulnerable
'How could you do this to me!'
—You react with utter hysteria

I'm no God
I'm simply
your mirror

16th.Apr.2016.   in Guangzhou

鏡子

我尖酸刻薄
我無中生有
我橫衝直撞
我目中無人

我道貌岸然
我陽奉陰違
我笑裏藏刀
我厚顏無恥

我冷漠如同雪上加霜
我輕蔑如同銀針穿刺皮肉
我狂怒如同颱風席捲
我攻擊如同瘋癲野獸

"你為何這樣傷害我……"
——你楚楚可憐
"你憑什麼如此對我！"
——你歇斯底里

我不是上帝
我不過是
你的鏡子

2016.4.16.　　　　於 廣州

Hesitation

I walked through the door
you looked towards me
A moment of hesitation
flashed in your eyes
I then understood
over these years, my
growing aging and frailty

15th.May.2016.   in Beijing

遲疑

我走進門
你看向我
目光中閃過
瞬間的遲疑
我便明白了
這些年，我的
衰老與軟弱

2016.5.15.   於 北京

Cure

Ignite a fire, burning away
Desires scream
Desires flutter like joss papers in the underworld
From this heavy snowfall
discard the flames themselves
You depart without a trace
You almost speak, telling me:
this is growth
and this is the cure

17th.Oct.2015.　　in London

治愈

燃一把火燒毀
慾望在尖叫
慾望似冥幣紛飛
從這場大雪開始
丟棄火焰本身
你絕塵而去
你幾乎就要開口，告訴我：
這就是成長
這便是治愈

2015.10.17.　　於 倫敦

Days without Poetry

Days without poetry
why bother walking around streets and alleys
and dressing up yourself?
Just a pile of organs
dressed up in glamour
in the emptiness, to spend a long while

8th.Jul.2015.　　　in London

無詩可寫的日子

無詩可寫的日子
何必走街串巷，添置新裳？
不過華麗裝扮了
一組器官
在虛空中，消磨半晌

2015.7.8. 於 倫敦

Emptiness

The days without poetry
your heart, is empty
To walk at a slower pace
lift your skirt hem, and climb the stairs
The time spent sitting in the park in silence
is like a rising smoke ring
Be in a daze in the library for half a day
the old man next seat—
the sound of his newspaper flipping
makes you want to take
a long nap
And also–
Those stone pavements—
the click-clack sounds of high heels
Those underground trains coming and going—
the bangs tilted by winds
Those waitings—
the extremely boring TV series
Those short-lived surprises—
the psychedelic on the journeys
Those tiresome construction noises…
Those and these, these and those…
Luckily no one asks you:
what is the meaning of life?
This wasted time...
A burnt-out candle, perhaps
is just so

29th.Jun.2015.   in London

虛空

無詩可寫的日子
你的胸中，空空蕩蕩
放慢步伐行走
提起裙角，爬升階梯
公園裏靜坐的時間
似裊裊上升的煙圈
圖書館中放空半日
隔壁座位的老頭
他翻動報紙的聲音
令你想長長地
睡上一覺
還有——
那些石板路
高跟鞋的"咯咯"聲
那些地鐵往來
被風吹斜的劉海
那些等待
窮極無聊的電視劇
那些短暫的驚喜
旅程中的迷幻藥
那些燥熱的施工聲
那些這些，這些那些
幸好沒有人考問你:
生之意義何在?
這虛度的光陰呵……
一支燃盡的蠟燭
大概也不過如此

2015.6.29.　　　　於 倫敦

A Day in Early May

It's so hot
I'm reading poetry in the café
with an iced latte in front of me
Except love
there's nothing in this world worth of nostalgia
People have numb faces
The scars suffered in the past
have become the marks in life
become the tracks of growth
My heart is an expanse of greyness
I haven't known the taste of happiness for long
not even pleasure
I can't hide from myself
Awakening my senses, the café
is playing age-old tunes, evoking
a world-weariness

6th.May.2016.   in Guangzhou

五月初的一天

如此炎熱
我在咖啡館裏讀詩
面前擺放著一杯冰拿鐵
除了情感
這世上沒有什麼值得留戀
人們長著一張張麻木的臉
過去遭受的傷痕
變成生命中的刻印
變成成長的軌跡
我的心中一片灰色
已很久不知快樂的滋味
甚至並無快感
我無法躲避自己
回過神，咖啡館裏播放著
年代久遠的輕音樂
令人厭世

2016.5.6.　於　廣州

Filling

Sleepy, walking dead, with a man in a bar
eighteen years old whiskey, Davidoff cigars
'The conversation goes on.' Time and space turn upside down
air feculent, nostalgic music wafting in the room
A thick cloud of smoke exhaled of
her mouth, instantly disappeared, a ghost
The conversation goes on. To talk about poetry
human nature, or other things
In the hollow of life, the conversation
must go on
like filling a wound

5th.Aug.2016.   in Shenzhen

填補

困倦，行屍走肉，與一個男人在酒吧裏
十八年的威士忌，大衛杜夫牌雪茄
"交談下去。"時空顛倒
空氣混沌，屋內飄蕩著懷舊音樂
口中噴出
濃厚的一簇煙霧，瞬間無蹤，幽靈
交談下去。談論詩歌
人性，或其他
在生命的空洞裏必須交談下去
像填補一個傷口

2016.8.5.　　　　　於 深圳

Exposure

Passengers on London Underground trains
always hold a piece of newspaper
a book or something in their hands
reading silently, during the journey
The Asian girl with long black hair
sitting next to me today
was also holding a book
She turned to a page and
it was full of—
Chinese Characters!
The language, exposed in an instant
her identity
And my heart, was in an instant
softened

6th.Jul.2015.   in London

曝露

倫敦地鐵上的乘客們
習慣手捧
一張報紙，一本書
旅途中，無聲閱讀
今天坐在我旁邊的
黑色長髮，亞洲女孩
也捧一本書
她翻開中間一頁
滿篇的——
中、國、漢、字、
語言，在瞬間曝露了
她的身份
我的心，在瞬間
柔軟

2015.7.6. 於 倫敦

Clown

Poetry is a gift from suffering
The moment your heart falls from the chest cavity
you understand this
Emp—ty
Every—thing
You squint your eyes
unable to face the brilliant weather of the past few days
Is this a disdain for the world, or a reluctant yearning?
Your pupils dilate,
spread—out—
unrestrainedly spreading
as if losing control, they scatter—
It can be sure that you are not on drugs
and for a long year
you haven't even touched a drop of alcohol
But now, your limbs are restless
jumping, shaking
An absurd and funny clown
But you have no other way
Don't know what to do
Don't know what to do
And you have no other way
The sun is shining outside the window—
under the sun, each person clings to a sweet dream
You dread hearing those dreams crash
breaking with a crisp, fracturing sound
Sometimes, it's thought
your heart is the tenderest of all
Under the sun, each holds a sweet dream
why then, must you play the part
of a wheezing, struggling poet of pain?

Po—et
thinking of this word, your mouth corners raise slightly
You spread your ten fingers, facing a piece of blank paper
Snow white
The forefinger, trembling, yet never pressing down
is your suppressed, secret desire
You feel you've exhausted all your thoughts and words
How you worry that you will lose the ability to write poems
A couple of days ago, for a moment
you thought about using a whole pack of sleeping pills
to end your sorrow
and fear—yes, you have that too
boundless, endless fear
Would a whole pack be enough?
You asked yourself
But after all, you didn't accomplish a thing
You didn't even accomplish—death
Now, you're sitting right here
ten fingers extended, facing a piece of snow-white paper

10th.Apr.2015.   in London

155th

小丑

詩歌是苦難賦予的禮物
心臟從胸腔打落的瞬間
你明白了這一點
空 ——了
一 ——切
你將眼睛眯成兩條縫
無法直視兩三天以來晴朗至極的好天氣
是對這塵世的厭倦，抑或留戀？
你的瞳孔散開
散——開——
肆無忌憚地散開
像喪失控制力那樣，散——開——
可以確定你沒有磕藥
長久的一年裏
你甚至滴酒不沾
可這會兒你的四肢卻無法安於現狀
跳動，晃動
一名荒誕滑稽的小丑
而你別無他法
無所適從
無所適從
而你別無他法
窗外陽光明媚——
陽光下的每個人，都懷揣一個美夢
你多不願聽到美夢墜地
"哢嚓"的碎裂聲
有時人們認為
你有這世上最軟的心腸
陽光下的每個人，都懷揣一個美夢
你又何苦再做個
吭哧吭哧的苦行詩人

詩——人
想到這個詞，你嘴角微微向上翹了翹
你將十指張開，面對一頁白紙
雪白
長久抖動卻遲遲沒有按下的食指
是你壓抑隱秘的欲望
你感到理屈詞窮
你多麼擔心自己喪失掉寫詩的能力
前兩天，有那麼一瞬間
你考慮過用一板安眠藥
去解決你的憂傷
還有恐懼——你也有
無邊無際的恐懼
一整板的安眠藥，夠不夠？
你這樣問自己
可你終究一事無成
連死亡，你也沒有幹成
現在，你就坐在這裏
十指張開，面對一頁雪白的紙

2015.4.10.　　　　於 倫敦

Early Morning

Another unmotivated 8:00a.m.
I woke up
In the dream I felt so close to death
Dreams don't lie
Now awake
crawl out of warm covers
light the first cigarette of the day
undraw the blackout curtains
Sunlight casts a golden illusion on cornered objects
while the rest remain in deep, silent shadows
Looking out from my window
I see a construction worker sitting in a digger
circling, directing the machine
scooping earth here, then there
here, then there
And the sound of hammers on wood
machinery roaring
Another day begins like this
My sorrow, boundless

4th.Nov.2014.   in London

清晨

又一個失去動機的 8:00 整
我醒來
在夢中我離死亡如此之近
夢不會撒謊
現在我醒來
從溫熱被子裏鑽出
點燃今天第一支煙
拉開純黑色遮光窗簾
陽光給角落裏的事物鍍上一層金色幻夢
其餘事物仍舊深陷靜謐的暗色調中
從正對我的窗口看去
工人坐在鏟土車裏
指揮車子一圈圈地來回轉
把土從這裏，鏟到那裏
再從這裏，鏟到那裏
還有工人捶打木板，傳來聲音
機器轟鳴
新的一天就這樣開始了
我的憂傷無邊無際

2014.11.4.　　於 倫敦

My Younger Sister

One night
a man in a greyish-white shirt, came to tell me
that once, I had
a younger sister
who died
after only three days of life
'She got infected at the slightest contact with germs'

In my dream last night
he came, to tell me this

1st.Oct.2014.   in London

我的妹妹

一個夜晚
穿灰白襯衫的男人，來告訴我：
原來我曾經
有個妹妹
出生三天
就夭折了
"她一接觸帶菌的東西就會感染"

昨天夜晚的夢裏
他來，這樣告訴我

2014.10.1.　　於 倫敦

No Accomplice

Die now!
and whispering such repeatedly
Crawling, squirming—by staying here
we could still lose, but you

are not an accomplice
Despite the initiator of this blood-red desire
you do not know, of this secretly planned
carnival. After the disillusion

promises break one by one, besides love
things are not spared either
Those collapsed, pave a gravel road

leading to hell or heaven, the judge
will face the most stoic silence
after the sufferers' fall

Rolling waves put on a coat
fail to carve
a single tear's mark

6th.Mar.2010.   in London

沒有同謀

現在就死去!
如此往復地呢喃著
匍匐，蠕動，在這裏
並不能不失去，但你

不是同謀
儘管成為血紅色欲望的始作俑者
你並不清楚，這秘密策劃的
極度狂歡，幻滅之後

起誓接連破碎，除愛情之外
亦未能倖免於難
瓦解的，鋪成了碎石子路

無論通向地獄或天堂，審判者
都面臨著罹難人
隕落之後最堅忍的沉靜

滾動的浪潮穿上外套
劃不出
一道淚痕

2010.3.6. 於 倫敦

Grey Umbrella

Your wings are still in shape
who broke them?
In a puddle of grey
grey mud, or stagnant water
you're paddling. After a rampant rain

what you just lost, is a wisp of
soul that once settled you. But
as life tells me, every abandonment
ought to have a good excuse. So
who was your master?

2nd.Apr.2010.   in London

灰傘

你羽翼尚豐滿
卻被誰折斷?
在一團灰色的
灰色的，泥漿，或積水中
搖擺你的槳，倡狂的雨過之後

你丟失的，是一縷
曾安置你的靈魂，但
生活對我說，每一次拋棄
都該有個好藉口。那麼
誰是你的主人?

2010.4.2. 於 倫敦

Falling for a Killer's Life

You insist on prying into the truth
only to find the truth gruesome
In the still of the night
I fall for a killer's life

Long to go to
many uninhabited lands
and scale with you
each solitary mountain peak

I say, humans are far more complex than mountains
no matter how high, a mountain is just that
It does not move
It does not move

I'm going to
form an intimate relationship with the wilderness
an intimate relationship with things
deeply
further deep

4th.Dec.2013.   in London

愛上殺手的人生

你硬要扒開真相去看
才發現真相血淋淋
夜深人靜
我愛上殺手的人生

想去
許許多多的無人領土
和你共攀
一座座孤獨的山峰

我說，人比山複雜多了
再高的山，它只是座山
它不會動
它不會動

我將要
和大自然發生親密關係
和物發生親密關係
深入
再深入

2013.12.4.　　　　　於 倫敦

Hotel Room Numbers I Stayed in,

Late Summer and Early Autumn, 2013

Shenzhen: 1705
Nanjing: 301
Changsha: 3512
Beijing: a Super 8 hotel room, forget the room number
Guangzhou: 1504
In Shenzhen again: 1915
Hong Kong: 604

I can't stop everything from slipping away second by second

(15th.Oct.2013.   location unrecorded)

2013 年夏末秋初，我住過的賓館房間號

深圳：1705
南京：301
長沙：3512
北京：一間速 8，房號忘了
廣州：1504
又到深圳：1915
香港：604

我留不住時時刻刻正在失去的一切

(2013.10.15.　地點不詳)

Parting

I boarded the train at 11:31am
A female passenger pushing two large suitcases
had blocked the aisle
I've now eaten a cheeseburger
finished an iced latte
feeling energetic but sorrowful
just like that female passenger
looks vigorous but full of fury
She took a seat to my right
The train departures
makes me want to cry

S-City fades into the distance
The air conditioning in the train car works fine
Three kids are causing chaos
with one crying nonstop
another screaming at the top of his lungs
and another jumping around, yelling:
'Mom, your feet stink!'
I start to read a poetry book, sometimes sleep
read a bit, then pause
sleep, then wake

2nd.Aug.2016.   on a high-speed train

離別

上火車的時間是上午 11:31
一人推兩只大箱子的女乘客
把過道堵住
我吃掉一份芝士漢堡
喝掉一杯冰拿鐵
精力充沛但心情憂傷
就像那個女乘客
生龍活虎但滿腹怨氣
她在我的右邊落座
火車啟動
我有落淚的衝動

S 城在離我們遠去
車廂裏的空調沒有壞
三個孩子在胡鬧
一個不停地哭
一個拼命尖叫
還有一個上躥下跳，並且大喊:
媽媽你的腳好臭!
我開始讀詩集，睡覺
讀讀停停
睡睡醒醒

2016.8.2.　於 某高鐵上

Dark Cloud

A dark cloud
now rises in my belly
a shadowy, enigmatic turmoil
People often asked me
'Do you fear the dark?'
You know
those contradictory
conflicting
those mysterious
deviant
But I've never been
one for 'tradition',
sometimes, even
despising it
Then, many say
'You seek perfection,
playing the faultless goddess.'
But truthfully
I care less and less
about it all
What on earth makes
a wife better than a whore
a priest better than a hypocrite
a cop better than a thief?
The thief yelled: Why you still care
your sense of shame!
So, what's 'good'
and what's 'bad'?
Is everything, then,
equal?
Yet, I do unrealistically hope

that people can find joy and happiness
unswayed by me
or anyone else
I've also heard that tale:
'Two wolves inside everyone,
whichever you feed, you fatten it'
I'm not stubbornly ignorant—
writing this poem seems
to prove just that
though my tone might seem
a bit too casual
A dark cloud
rises in my belly
And like a tightrope walker
I tread the middle
Clearly, I'm neither black
nor white
nor 'the (ambiguous and popular) grey'
I feel I bear
no specific color

29th.Jun.2013.   in London

黑色的雲

現在我的腹中騰起
一團黑色的雲
從前，不止一人問我：
你有，黑暗恐懼症嗎？
就是那些
矛盾的
衝突的
詭秘的
離經叛道的
可我向來
並非＂傳統＂之人
有時簡直
痛恨傳統
不止一人又對我說：
你在，追求完美
大白話是：
裝、女、神
事實上我
越來越
不在乎這一切
憑什麼
太太就一定比娼妓更好？
牧師就一定比偽教徒更好？
警察就一定比小偷更好？
小偷說：誰叫你們
還要臉！
所以，＂好＂
是什麼
＂壞＂呢？
所以，一切都是
平等，的嗎？

174th

但我確實，不切實際地希望
只要人們樂意
就能幸福愉快
不為我所動
不為其他人所動
我還聽過那個：
 "每個人心裏都有兩只狼
喂哪只、肥哪只"的故事
——我並非冥頑不化的
——似乎寫下這首詩
就是為了證明
這一點
儘管語氣聽上去
過於隨便
現在我的腹中騰起一團
黑色的雲
我像個走鋼絲的人
踩在中間
我明明既不是黑色
也不是白色
也不是流行語所說的
 "灰色的"
我覺得我沒有什麼
特定的顏色

2013.6.29.　　　　　於　倫敦

Lullaby

Then perish for a moment
or sleep, prolonged and deep

The unspoken tabu
silence on the flames
briefly, may be harmonious

Oh listen, darling
be innocent
bleed white

9th.Mar.2012.   in London

搖籃曲

那就死上一會兒
或者長長地睡眠

未言明的戒律
火焰上的寂靜
有片刻表裏如一

噢聽著，親愛的
要天真無邪
流白色的血

2012.3.9. 於 倫敦

Dance Whirls

Pale, pale blue ocean
is an endless expanse of sky
Clouds parade by, as if
a secretly joyous group dance
Dum cha cha dum
then I truly see a rainbow
Before its spectral arc fades away—

lead me in a dance too
whirling steps, as if without friction

25th.Oct.2011.　　in London

舞步飛旋

淡藍淡藍的海洋
是了無邊際的天空
雲的隊伍遊過，似
一支暗自快樂的群舞
咚恰恰咚
而後我真的看見了彩虹
在那幻影的弧度消逝以前——

也牽我跳支舞吧
舞步飛旋，就像沒有摩擦力

2011.10.25.　　於 倫敦

Sickness. Spring Breeze Brings the Drizzle.

Needing a sickness
fevering limbs, help me
betray my rationality
a sore throat, helps me
ignore other
pains
Pills, tap water, toilet seat
you see, I even forget
to eat
Needing a sickness
spring breeze brings the drizzle, making me
clean
and, soft

7th.Mar.2013.   in London

疾病．春風化雨．

需要一場疾病
肢體滾燙，助我
背叛思想
咽喉腫痛，助我
忽視其他
疼痛
藥丸，白水，馬桶蓋
你看我甚至忘了
要吃飯
需要一場疾病
春風化雨，使我
乾淨
並且，柔軟

2013.3.7.　於　倫敦

Self-Immolation

The desire for freedom and love
was so intense that
I had burnt myself
to death
In the dying slumber
only dreams of despair

It's time to quit drinking
I scare myself

5th.Sep.2017.   in Guangzhou

自焚

對自由和愛的
欲望如此強烈
我把自己
燒死了
在瀕死的睡眠中
都是絕望的夢

我該戒酒了
我讓自己感到害怕

2017.9.5.   於 廣州

Just as

I fervently guard
your
—selfhood
just as I fiercely protect
mine

5th.Apr.2013.   in London

正如

我竭力保護
你們的
——自我
正如我竭力保護
我的

2013.4.5.   於 倫敦

Solitude

To wrap you all in pristine sheets
like perfect statues
I, bare and exposed
embrace each one
like a child

7th.Aug.2013.   in London

孤獨

為你們裹上潔白的床單
如一尊尊完美雕像
我赤身裸體
——擁抱
像個孩子

2013.8.7. 於 倫敦

Sometimes I'm the Ocean

also the forest and the sun
So determined believing
far from self-deceit
Gases swell
fluids flow
in my chest, a hammer pounds
forging a second life of my heart
Intermittently, the world appears agreeable
secure and enduring
Now, I can take a walk
into the bustling crowd
and perform an invulnerable

1st.Feb.2012.   in London

有時我是海

也是森林和太陽
如此堅決地相信
和自欺欺人沒有關係
氣體在膨脹
液體在流動
胸口一只鐵錘擊打
鑄成心的第二條命
世界間歇性順眼
安全且不朽

這會兒能去散散步
走進熙攘的人群
表演刀槍不入

2012.2.1. 於 倫敦

Such a Village

I swear it's true
I've thought it through
if ever fortune comes my way

I'll build a village
facing the sea, bathed in sunlight
And you all, yes, you all
will come
sing, dance, write poetry
drink, run, laugh aloud

And hands over hearts of our souls
we'll declare: every fairytale born of goodness
and its legitimacy
Regardless, we remain pure

Everybody loves everybody
day and night
Let's just be together, so

After contemplation

life goes on as usual
like the song's now singing:
farewells and death
just like now, I haven't
actually made a fortune

It isn't a surprise...

Simply
time passes, and I'm still not wealthy
nor is there
such a village

5th.Oct.2011.   in London

什麼村莊

我發誓是真的
前後想過
萬一發財的日子

就建一座村莊
面朝大海，充滿陽光
而你們，而你們
統統來了
歌唱，舞蹈，寫詩
飲酒，奔跑，大聲笑

還要，將手掌覆蓋靈魂的胸膛

宣告：一切以善出發的童話
及其合法性
無論如何，我們始終純潔

所有人同所有人相愛
日日夜夜
就這樣在一起吧，那麼

想過之後
一切如常
就像眼下，歌裏在唱：
告別和死亡
就像眼下，我還
沒有發財

倒也並無意外呵……

無非
歲月流逝，我還沒有發財
也沒有
什麼村莊

2011.10.5.　　　　於 倫敦

Writing on the Christmas Afternoon, 2013

I opened a novel with the intention of reading it
hoping that one day, I could also write something damn fascinating
I opened a novel with the intention of reading it

but quickly closed it paranoidly
These days I always behave against myself
the more I want to do something, the more skeptical I get
for example, I deliberately make myself think—
Why can't I
just live in a mess
awfully, disorderly?
In truth, it's hard to prove that all isn't just equal
Is it our fears that play tricks on us?
Perhaps there's no need to strive for
some perfectly fitting reasons
to justify the various choices
and grant them legitimacy
At this time, Y. was sitting on the sofa next to me
too bored to keep his eyes open
The magazine he was holding was more of a decoration
'You fancy reading on the balcony?' I asked
He glanced wearily towards the French window
London in winter
this quiet Christmas
'No.'
He thought the balcony too chilly
I, however, longed to try
bundled up in a heavy coat
reading a book on the balcony
Falling for a cold passion
like the Japanese Sake

25th.Dec.2013.   in London

寫在2013年聖誕節下午

我翻開一本小說打算閱讀
希望自己有朝一日，也能寫出牛逼小說
我翻開一本小說打算閱讀
卻又神經質地合上
如今我總和自己做對
越是想做的事情，就越是抱以懷疑態度
比方我有意讓自己思考——
憑什麼我
不能過成一灘爛泥
過得一塌糊塗，亂七八糟？
事實上你很難證明：一切不是平等的
是我們的恐懼在作祟嗎？
是不是也沒必要，企圖找出什麼
恰如其分的理由
好讓種種選擇
獲得其合法性
這時候Y就坐在緊挨我的沙發上
他無聊得睜不開眼
他手裏捧的雜誌更像是一種裝飾
"你想坐在陽臺上看書嗎"，我問
他無精打采地看向落地窗外
倫敦的冬天
這個靜謐的聖誕節
"不想。"
他覺得陽臺上太冷了
其實我很想嘗一嘗
裹著厚大衣
待在陽臺上看書
的滋味
愛上一種清冷的激情
像日本人的清酒

2013.12.25. 　於 倫敦

Attempted

Summer was here in London
sky so blue
so blue that
we wanted to murder it

Go ahead, you said. Slight twitch
of the innocent eyelashes
I did bring the kitchen knife
but in the end, you and I achieved nothing

Later on
dark clouds, like spilled ink, stained the sky
I had no choice but to watch the relentless rain
and wonder, annoyed:
between murder and attempted murder, who on earth
is braver?

Now the sky is, half grey half blue
and I, like most happy people
cannot tell

But I'm faking my happiness

12th.Jun.2011.　　　in London

未遂

倫敦的夏天來了
天空藍得要命
藍得
我們想謀殺它

你說：去吧。微微抖動
無辜的眼睫毛
我當真拿來菜刀
可最終，我倆一事無成

後來
烏雲像墨汁，染了天空
不得不看雨點劈哩啪啦，使我
懊惱地想了想:
謀殺或者謀殺未遂，究竟
誰更勇敢?

現在的天，半灰半藍的
我像大多數的快樂者
分辨不出

可我的快樂是裝的

2011.6.12.　　　　於 倫敦

Tailor

I've journeyed through tangled sceneries, and I
never regretted it
Punctured youth sometimes leaks, then grab
handfuls of life's smokescreens
stitching and mending

23rd.Jul.2010.   in London

裁縫

我曾穿越繚亂景色，我
從未悔過
戳破的青春
有時漏風，便
抓一把生活的煙幕
縫縫補補

2010.7.23.   於 倫敦

Samsara

You saw how I died

and came back to life
In this cycle of life and death
how many times I have gone through
heart-piercing sentimentality

This current age
leaves us numb
but I still feel:
when you reach deep inside of me
I still taste and smell:
white mist through my nostrils
thudding into my lungs

and I still hear:
I hear you laughing hollowly, moaning hollowly, weeping
hollowly in the festering blue lotus

The old tree's trembling
from the cold, or the joy of hearing waltz?
Once more, a line divides the sky into black and white
and the sun is like a passerby, gifting me a string of fantasies

Then it shatters
something unknown hits the ground
A lane that curves into countless turns is called a road

He makes a sound
she makes a sound
someone found a way on the edge of the ocean
and an ocean on the edge of a way

How come I float on water like this?
asking, as if I were a brave woman

Is the allure of a smile
merely a mask for inner turmoil?
A show colder than the cold times?

Faking is my talent
Yours too, isn't it?
Isn't it?

I haven't yet run away
for bravery is yet to find me

18th.Oct.2005.   in Newcastle, UK

輪回

你們看見我怎樣死去
又蘇醒過來
在這樣的生死輪回之中
我經歷了多少次
撕心裂肺的感傷

正在發生的這個時代
已令人麻木
然而我依然有觸覺：
當你探入深處的瞬間
我依然有味覺與嗅覺：
白色的霧穿過鼻孔
"咚"地落進肺裏

我也還有聽覺：

我聽見你們在藍蓮花的潰爛裏空洞地笑
空洞地呻吟與流淚

老樹在震顫
因為寒冷，或是聽見華爾茲的喜悅
天空又是黑與白的一線之隔
陽光如同路人甲，施捨我一串幻想

然後碎了
不知是什麼打落在地上
彎成無數個彎的小道被人們稱為馬路

他發出聲音
她發出聲音
有人在海洋的邊境找到了路
又在路的邊境找到海洋

我怎會像這樣漂在水上？
這樣問，仿佛我又成了一個勇者

魅惑的笑
是否就掩蓋了內心的慌？
那是否寒冷之際更為寒冷的一次表演？

表演是我的天賦
也是你的吧？
也是你的吧？

我沒有逃
因為還不夠勇敢

2005.10.18.　　於 英國，紐卡斯爾

194th

Windows All Locked

Alone, my heart races
Head spins, limbs numb then regain feeling
I visited the doctor
who, after hearing just a sentence, said:
'Isn't this a psychological issue...'
Still, I'm prescribed
blood-activating and stasis-removing painkillers
for 'chest pain, heartache, dizziness', etc.
Maybe I should cut down on medicines
my memory isn't what it used to be now
Besides:
over-pampering the body isn't good
You smile at it ninety-nine times, and the hundredth time you don't
it slaps you
I intend to secretly cut down my meds (behind the doctor's back)
My mum was mad at me yesterday
mad at me, again
even though we seem to be on the same page when
it comes to reducing meds
But she was not satisfied
she's always dissatisfied
She said I broke her heart, again
She said that being with me was just asking for trouble
blablabla, again
She got Dad to be the lobbyist, again and again and again
They always play this card
becoming a lobbying buddy for each other
and I'm like the middle of a sandwich, or of a sandwich biscuit
Every day, too easy to find something to be unhappy about
Frankly
I don't want to hurt her at all; do you believe me?

It doesn't actually matter whether you believe me or not
I just DON'T—WANT—TO—HURT—HER, at all
At the moment of parting, my face was tight, stretched long
and now I sit alone in this huge hotel room, crying
On the eighteenth floor of the hotel
the windows are all locked
and I can almost hear my own pulse
The hotelier has probably seen too many...
...lunatics like me
and is afraid we would jump off the building
Anyway, the windows won't open
Anyway, it's f*cking quiet
Oh now, here comes the cleaning lady
she's ringing the doorbell outside

16th.Jun.2014.   in Shenzhen

窗戶全鎖上了

一個人待著，心慌
頭暈，四肢迅速麻木，又恢復知覺
去看醫生
醫生只聽我說了一句，就說：
你這是心理問題吧……
仍給我開了些活血化淤，通絡止痛的藥
用於：
"胸痹，心痛，眩暈"，等等
我倒是該少吃點兒藥
記憶力大不如前
另外：

把身體養得過分嬌貴，總歸不是件好事
你對它笑了九十九次，第一百次沒有笑
它就給你一巴掌
我想嘗試自己偷偷減藥（背著醫生）
昨天媽媽生我氣了
又生我氣了
儘管在減藥這個問題上，我們似乎意見一致
但她不滿意
她總是不滿意
她說我又傷了她的心，又
她說和我待在一塊兒是自找不痛快云云，又
她找爸爸來做我的說客，又又又
他倆總是這樣，互為對方的說客
我像三明治的中間層，或者夾心餅乾
想每天找出點兒不高興的事兒太容易了
其實吧
我一點兒也不想傷害她你相信嗎
你信不信也不重要
我就是一點兒，也不想，傷、害、她
我在分離的一刻臉繃得緊緊的拉得老長
現在我獨自一人坐在酒店寬大的房間裏流淚
酒店的第十八層
窗戶全被鎖上了
我幾乎聽見自己的脈搏聲
酒店經營者大概是見多了我這樣的女神……
……經
生怕我們往下跳
總之窗戶打不開
總之真他媽安靜
噢現在，清潔工來了
她在門外按著門鈴

2014.6.16.　　　　於 深圳

In Psychiatric Ward

1. In Psychiatric Ward

A girl with yellowish
dusky skin
sits sideways
perched on a chair's armrest
Long bangs fall down
She peers at me through her fingers
cautiously, reservedly

2. Notes of a Bipolar Patient

I live in a mental hospital
trying to document something
My constant effort to record
Humans desire for immortality

I don't want to be part of their games
the medication in exchange makes my head heavy
I sleep, and sleep, and sleep
These days I spend so much time sleeping
I'm scared I might just sleep through my life
Turns out, I'm also afraid of death

It's hard to let go
There are so many things left unfinished
so much love left uncompleted
so I must keep holding on
living to love, to create

You have to convince yourself
that everyone is here to help
If you think that way
things might just turn out that way
Try it—
stay sober, close your eyes, lean back
as if there's no gravity
Trust that they will catch you
accept you. Love is the only way

If you hate being asleep
then cherish every moment of consciousness
Oh, my ten fingers, meant for creating
how could them be wasted on petty disputes?

I live in a mental hospital
trying to document something
The boy next room thinks he's in a prison
obsessed with
the plastic tag on our wrists with our name,
age, gender, and department
This boy can recite ancient Chinese poems
he recites Li Bai's 'Moonlight there is afore My Bed' (床前明月
光)
and came to ask, if I could teach him more ancient poems
Another gorgeously dressed girl
dresses up every day
pacing back and forth in the long corridor of the hospital
seems lost in thought
Don't understand, how come the nurses tolerate her for not
wearing a patient gown
There is also an old woman who knocks on my door late at night
claims wishing to make friends with me

she doesn't wear a patient gown either
instead wearing a bright red jacket, sunglasses at late night
'Can I come in and sit for a while? I want to make friends with you.'
she says to me
She has indeed scared me
and she comes again and again, 'I feel being linked with you by fate.'
She really wants me to open my mouth and talk
but hell no, I don't even know her
There are a lot more things

I'm staying in a mental hospital
trying to record something
For the first time, I feel so close to death
I even start to think
after death, who should help
to publish my works
Honestly, I should be scared of my own writing
I love it so much
that love, even surpasses, the act of writing itself
Sometimes for long, I dare not pick up a pen
fear ruining its perfection once I start writing
I'm afraid I will be burned by it, devoured by it
I'm afraid I will be burned by it

The feeling of burning is exact
no one knows this exact feeling better than me
But now I want to live
I've never wanted it so strongly before
Now I will live
for a long, long time
to love, to create, and to live well

200th

3. Just Write

I want to write
just write
Before I become a real mad person
I need to leave behind something
or leave more, while my sensitive nerves still exist
Interesting, when I attempted to type 'disappear' in pinyin (1)
the laptop input has associated the word 'hour'
It also knows, all this has something to do with time
'Elapse' is also related to time (2)
Perhaps I won't be an exceptional writer
and this saddens me
My writing lacks planning, too random
is relying solely on passion unreliable?
Should I pay attention to the footsteps in the hospital's long
corridor?
Is that wrong?
My parents wish I'd think less
be sunnier
and happier
Y. wishes so too
I typed 'sunnier' and 'happier'
the laptop says 'almost' (2)
I'm waiting
I'm waiting
Now the sky is dark
with impending rain
muffled thunders
I remember loving these moments as a child
this sensation, heavy rain in broad daylight
and I sat quietly in my room, doing something
feeling safe

I'll rid myself of this eerie sensation
better to forget it all
Just live well
I love this world so much

(1) Pinyin (拼音) is the Romanization of the Chinese characters based on their pronunciation. In Mandarin Chinese, the phrase 'Pin Yin' literally translates into 'spell sound.' In other words, spelling out Chinese phrases with letters from the English alphabet.
(2) The word 'disappear (消失)', 'hour (小时)' and 'elapse (消逝)' have similar pronunciations in Chinese language; so do 'happy (快乐)' and 'almost (快了)'.

4. Survived in Death Line

No silly trying, no stupid dying
—my medical report made it perfectly clear
Something went wrong, seemingly hepatitis B
The doctor was relieved that
my antigen was negative
although my antibodies, absurdly high
—normal is around 10
I had over 300
My mother said it meant
hepatitis B waged a war inside me
and my body fought back
won, and left these antibodies
The doctor said high antibodies are good
a sign of strong resistance to the disease
But it still means
I was once infected the hepatitis B disease
Survived in death line
a frightening thought

How can I live better?
Consistently inept at the daily life
Relax
Relax
Am I not holding on too tight?

5. Dismal Life of Smokers

I want to hide by the only open window at the end of the hospital corridor
to smoke a cigarette
but there are too many people, they're doing exercises
stretching arms, stretching legs, whatever
I thought even though they were stretching their arms and legs or whatever
nobody would walk to the window, so deep
But a big guy comes over
it's like, he has already seen through my conspiracy
I want to smoke a cigarette in the small garden on the sixth floor of the hospital
but there are signs everywhere in the small garden:
smoke-free hospital, smoking is prohibited here, and so forth
The small garden is just facing the one after another doctor's office room with their windows wide open
Damn it
Anyway, I could smoke on the first floor
There is big empty space for parking and reversing cars there
I go for a walk with Y. whenever I get the chance
happy like a king, for a little while
The problem is
it's too troublesome to go to the first floor:
I need to lock the room door—too many patients are staying along the corridor

and I don't have the key
This means after the door is locked
just five minutes after I step downstairs for a smoke
I would rush back up, pester the nurse for the key
and if I keep doing this
I will drive the nurse crazy
Finally, I decide to hide in the toilet in my ward to smoke
I take a disposable plastic cup
pour in some water
it then becomes a perfect ashtray
The cigarette butts I secretly smoked the last few times
are lying quietly in the cup now
The butts are soaked, and the water has become yellow
like a kind of pleasant psychedelic
I pick up this cup again
lock myself in the toilet
wolf down my cigarette
I keep inhaling until the filter tip burning hot
oh, damn sweet

6. Every Person on the Sixth-Floor Terrace is like a Long Take

Every person on the sixth-floor terrace is like a long take
There is a small garden on the sixth floor of the hospital
but I prefer to call it: the big terrace
open-air, a romantic way to call it
People on the sixth-floor terrace
they're always walking slowly
going in circles, or pacing in a same place
Anyway, they're slow, slowly
Some exercise, rooted in one spot
arms swinging in crisscross, pounding their shoulders
or stepping one foot after another on the flower bed's edge

alternating steps, picking up speed until it turns into a bounce
There is also an old gentleman who plays badminton
The first time, he saw me and Y. sitting on the stone steps beside
he said to me: 'You two are so happy! You'll heal fast!'
He also suggested me to smoke less
I've seen him twice playing badminton on the sixth-floor open
terrace
The second time his sister came
sister lulled him and said: you can leave the hospital tomorrow,
how great!
Sister wanted him to do more outdoor exercises, play badminton or
something else
Sister was gone, the old man hugged her tightly before she left
Others saw his sister gone, asked the nurse:
Will he be discharged tomorrow?
The young nurse shook his head with a heavy look
when the old man turned to the other way
and bent down to
pick up a badminton that
fell on the floor
Every person on the sixth-floor terrace is like a long take
Sometimes I sit on the long stone steps on the edge of the terrace
there sit two irrelevant strangers beside
taken off their shoes, barefoot, light a cigarette
using their home dialect to talk about something
Their home dialect is very much like Hokkien
but I can't be sure
And there is an old lady in wheelchair
brings a radio of her own
rustling sounds from the radio, and there is music
all kinds of old Chinese songs
very much like going back in time
So damn romantic
So damn romantic

Every person on the sixth-floor terrace
is like a long take

7. Untitled

I've realized no truths from poetry
My self-destructive desires so profound, and heavy
never fading
Yet love, creation
love, a return journey to
our life—right now
this thought surpasses everything else

May 2014   in Guangzhou

在精神科

1. 在精神科

黃黃的
黝黑皮膚的姑娘
側身坐在
椅子扶手上
長劉海垂下來
她從指縫間看我
謹慎地，內斂地

2. 躁鬱症患者手記

我在精神病院裏住著
企圖記錄一些什麼
我總在企圖記錄
人們渴望著不朽

我不願參與，他們的遊戲
換來的藥物使頭腦沉重
昏睡，昏睡，昏睡
這些天我在昏睡中度過許多時間
真害怕就這樣睡了過去
原來，我也是懼怕死亡的

太不舍了
還有那麼多未完成的事情
未完成的愛
所以就得，活下去
活下去，去愛，去創造

妳務必使自己相信
每一個人，都是來幫助妳的
妳這樣想
事情就會真的朝這個方向發展
試一試
清醒，閉目，全力以赴地向後躺倒
像沒有重力
妳要相信他們正在身後接著妳
接納妳，唯有愛

而妳若厭惡昏睡
就要珍惜清醒的每一刻
我那用於創造的十指啊

怎能以它們，搬弄是非

我在精神病院裏住著
企圖記錄一些什麼
隔壁房間的男孩一心認為自己住進了監獄
他耿耿於懷的是
每個人右手腕上系著一根塑膠紙條
那上面有我們的名字
年齡，性別，還有科室
這個男孩會背古詩
他背誦李白的"床前明月光"
還來詢問我，是不是能教給他更多古詩
另一個穿著華麗的女孩
每日盛裝，在醫院的長走廊上來回踱步
若有所思
弄不懂，護士怎能容忍她不穿病號服
還有一位夜裏來敲我房門
聲稱要和我交朋友的老大媽
她也不穿病號服
大晚上穿著大紅色外套，戴墨鏡
"我能進來坐一會兒嗎？我想和你做朋友"
她對我說
她著實把我給嚇著了
她並且三番五次地來，"我感覺和你很有緣份啊"
她一定要我張嘴說話
可我就不，我又不認識她
還有很多

我在精神病院裏住著
企圖記錄一些什麼
第一次，我感到自已離死亡如此之近
我甚至開始考慮
死亡之後，將由誰誰來完成
我的作品出版

208th

說真的，我應當害怕自己寫作的樣子
我是如此熱愛它
以至於，愛，甚至多過於，寫，本身
我久久不敢落筆
擔心自己一旦動筆就破壞掉它的完美性
我害怕自己被它燒掉，被它吃掉
我害怕自己被它燒掉

燃燒的感覺是確切的
沒有誰比我更懂得這個確切的感覺
但是現在我想要活下去
前所未有的強烈願望
現在我要活下去
很久，很久
去愛，去創造，去好好生活

3. 想寫

想寫
就是想寫
我要趁我變成真正的精神病人之前多留下些什麼
或者，在我的敏感神經消失之前
多留下些什麼
真有意思，當我企圖用拼音打下"消失"
電腦輸入法裏聯想出了"小時"二字
它也知道，這一切與時間有關
"消逝"也與時間有關
我也許不會成為一名優秀的寫作者
我這樣悲傷地感到
我的寫作太缺乏計劃性，隨機性太強
一味地憑藉激情寫作是不是不可靠？
我會去注意醫院長走道上的腳步聲
這是不是不好？

我的父母希望我想得更少一些
陽光一些
快樂一些
Y.也是如此
我打下"陽光"和"快樂"
電腦說"快了"
我等待著
我等待著
現在天黑了
一場下不下來的雨
悶雷的聲音
我記得小時候最愛
這種大白天裏昏天黑地下大雨的感覺
自己安靜地坐在房間裏幹點兒什麼
就覺得安全
我會把靈異的感覺從自己身上去除掉
以後乾脆忘掉這一切吧
就是好好活著
我那麼愛這世界

4. 死而後生

不作死就不會死
我的體檢報表充分地
說明了這一點
出了一些毛病，似乎是乙肝
醫生說好在
抗原是陰性的
就是抗體多得不像話
正常數值好像應該是 10 幾
可我有 300 多
我媽說，這說明
乙肝疾病曾在我的體內打了一仗

我的身體跟它抗衡
然後身體打贏了，就留下了這些抗體
醫生說，抗體多是好事
說明對於乙肝疾病的抵抗力強
可這畢竟說明
我曾經感染過乙肝
死而後生
這真是讓人後怕
我要怎樣，才能過活得更好一些？
我總是這樣不善於過生活
放鬆一些
放鬆一些
抓得太緊了吧

5. 煙民們的慘淡生活

我想躲在醫院樓道盡頭唯一一扇開著的窗那兒
抽支煙
結果人太多了，人們紛紛在做運動
抻抻胳膊，抻抻腿，什麼的
我本以為即使他們在抻抻胳膊抻抻腿什麼的
沒有人會走到窗邊，這麼深
結果一個彪形大漢走了過來
就好像，他早已識破我的陰謀
我想在醫院六樓的小花園裏抽支煙
結果小花院裏到處立著標誌：
無煙醫院，此處禁止吸煙，云云
小花園就正對著一間間窗戶敞開的醫生辦公室
真是可惡
一樓倒是可以抽煙的
那兒有一大片停車，倒車用的空地
一有機會我就和 Y.下去散步
快活似神仙，那麼一小會兒

問題是
要去一樓太麻煩：
得鎖門，樓道裏的住客太多了
而我沒有鑰匙
這就意味著在把門反鎖之後
在我下樓抽完煙的僅僅五分鐘之後
又得跑上樓向護士要鑰匙
如此形成慣例
護士會煩死我
最終我決定躲在房間的廁所裏抽
我拿了一只一次性使用的塑膠杯
裏邊倒上點兒水
就成了一只完美煙灰缸
前幾次我偷偷抽完的煙頭
現在就靜靜地躺在杯子裏
水已泡得發黃，仿佛一種愉悅的迷幻
再拿起這只杯子
把自己鎖在廁所裏
狼吞虎咽
我一直咂到過濾嘴兒都發燙了
真他媽香啊

6. 六樓陽臺上的每一個人，都像一個長鏡頭

六樓陽臺上的每一個人都像一個長鏡頭
醫院六樓有個小花園
而我更願稱之為：陽臺
露天的，浪漫的，叫法
六樓陽臺上的人們
他們總在慢慢地走著
兜圈子，或是原地踏步
總之就是慢慢地，慢慢地
一些人會做運動，站定一個地方

雙臂交錯擺動，捶打肩膀
或是一腳接一腳地踏著花壇護欄
也是交錯著踏，速度快起來就成了彈跳
還有一個打羽毛球的老先生
第一次時，他見到我和 Y.坐在一旁的石階上，
他對我說：“好幸福啊！這樣病肯定好得快！”
他還囑咐我少抽些煙
我見過他兩次在六樓的露天陽臺上打羽毛球
第二次時他的姐姐來了
姐姐欺哄他說：明天就可以出院了哦，多好呀
姐姐希望他多做戶外運動，打打羽毛球什麼的
姐姐走了，之前老先生使勁地擁抱她
旁人見姐姐走了就問小護工：
他明天就出院啦？
小護工趁老先生背轉身
神色凝重輕搖頭
老先生弓著背
揀起掉在地上的一只
羽毛球
六樓陽臺上的每一個人都像一個長鏡頭
有時我在陽臺邊緣的長石階上坐著
旁邊也坐不相干的兩個人
脫了鞋，光著腳丫子，點一支煙
拿家鄉話聊點兒什麼
他們的家鄉話很像閩南話
但我無法確定
還有輪椅上的老太太
自帶一個收音機
收音機裏滋滋拉拉，一會兒又響出音樂
酒幹倘賣無，十五的月亮，什麼的
像極了時光倒流
簡直浪漫死了
簡直浪漫死了
六樓陽臺上的每一個人

都像一個長鏡頭

7. 無題

我沒有從詩歌中悟出什麼道理
我的自毀之欲念如此深重
從未消去
然而愛啊，創造啊
愛啊，重新走向
我們的生活啊──眼下
這想法勝過了一切

2014.5. 於 廣州

Part Six: Ending | 第六輯 尾聲

Around Early Winter 2005

Ye and Tan came to visit me and Yang
(Back then, Tan was Ye's girlfriend)
(And I was Yang's girlfriend)
We chatted
until nearly 4 a.m.
when suddenly, Yang suggested watching the sunrise
So, in his old, second-hand Rover
(a dark blue one)
he drove the three of us
to the seaside of Newcastle, England

It was really cold on the winter's pre-dawn beach
I wore a coat of Yang's
as the wind whirring, rushed in and out
We were young and excited
taking photos in front of a graffiti wall
Yang even snapped one of me 'pinching' the sunrise
(back when he hadn't yet abandoned art for business)
(Until the summer of 2018, he took all my best photos)
We walked along the coastline
leaving a trail of footprints in the sand

Later, we bought eight crabs
(two each)
ginger and vinegar
While waiting for the supermarket in Chinatown to open
we dozed off in the car
Waking up, I rested my hands on the car's sunroof
and Tan took a photo of it
The black and red nail polish
was chipped and worn
but we thought it looked good

Back home, after eating the crabs, we slept
Tan and I in the bed
Yang and Ye on the floor in our sleeping bags
We slept so deeply
only waking in the evening when the landlord knocked
to have us sign for a parcel
Pulling back the curtains
the sky had completely darkened
This was around early winter 2005

By spring
Tan had run off with a married man who
owned a singers' agency
And after another six months
Yang and I also broke up

26th.May.2018.   in Shenzhen

大約是在 2005 年初冬

小葉和小譚來找我和小楊
　（當時小譚是小葉女友）
　（我是小楊女友）
我們聊天
快到臨晨四點鐘時
小楊突然說去看日出
於是開著他的二手破舊羅孚
　（深藍色的）
載著我們三人
往英格蘭紐卡斯爾的海邊去

冬天淩晨的海邊可真冷呀
我身上套一件小楊的大衣
風呼呼地來了又去
我們年輕並且興奮
在海邊一面塗鴉牆前照相
小楊又喊我捏著日出照了一張
　（那時小楊還沒放棄藝術變成商人）
　（至 2018 年夏天，我最棒的照片都是他拍的）
我們還沿著海岸線走了一會兒
在沙灘上踩出一長串腳印

後來買了八只螃蟹
　（每人兩只）
薑和醋
在唐人街等待超市開門時
大家在車裏迷糊了一會兒
醒來後我把手搭在汽車天窗上
小譚給我的手拍了張照片
黑色和紅色的指甲油
掉得七零八落

我們都覺得那樣子很好看

回到家吃完螃蟹就睡了
我和小譚在床上睡
小楊和小葉拿了我們的野營睡袋
在地上睡
那一覺睡得可真沉呀
直到傍晚房東來敲門
喊我們簽收郵件
拉開窗簾
天已經完全黑下來
這大約是在 2005 年初冬吧

等到春天的時候
小譚就跟一個開演藝公司的
有婦之夫跑了
又過了整整六個月
我和小楊也分手了

2018.5.26.　　　　於 深圳

Festival

The fear of the atmosphere leading up to any festival
outweighs the festival itself
much like the fear of death coming
outweighs death itself
When the day of Spring Festival actually arrives (1)
it's merely just so
Football can be played on
the empty streets
with occasional cars driving by
The breakfast cafe downstairs
opened until the 29th of the twelfth lunar month
which was quite a dedication
On the way I passed by
a security guard with a red armband was still on duty
we inexplicably said hi to each other
Starbucks founded by the Americans
is open 365 days a year
—how grateful I am at this moment
Inside, it's still playing music with a nomadic feel
and I'm still working with my laptop
as usual

15th.Feb.2018.   in Guangzhou

(1) Spring Festival (春節) is the traditional Chinese New Year.

節日

恐懼節日之前的氣氛
遠大於節日本身
就像對於死亡的恐懼
遠大於死亡本身
真到了春節這一天
無非也就如此了
空曠的街道上
可以踢足球
偶有零星車輛駛過
家樓下的早餐店
營業到臘月二十九
也算敬業
經過的路上
戴紅袖章的保安仍在執勤
我們莫名其妙地互道你好
美國人的星巴克
365 天全年無休
此刻我多麼心存感激
裏面仍舊播放著流浪感的音樂
我仍舊背著手提電腦工作
像往常一樣

2018.2.15.　　　　於 廣州

In the Festival of the World

You walk alone on the streets of the city
cold and lonely in the festival of the world
The homeless child
has now grown into a middle-aged woman
To escape from the family, you endure the hardship of an arduous
journey
At night you look in the cell phone to find someone who can
chitchat with
Always there are sincere and warmhearted people
trying to teach you the 'true meaning of life'
and they make your palms sweat
In the morning you
see loving fathers and filial sons
see perfect husbands and wives
and hear the vibrant sounds of cars
But you prefer those in the breakfast store
like you, solitary
in the pervasive festival atmosphere
scattered
alone
Trust me
if you're sober enough
will eventually be forsaken by this world
just as you've long forsaken it

6th.Feb.2018.   in Guangzhou

在世界的節日裏

你獨自行走於城市街道
在世界的節日裏清冷寂寥
無家可歸的孩子
如今長成中年女人
為躲避家庭你風餐露宿
夜晚翻查手機尋找可以閒聊的人
總有古道熱腸者
試圖教給你生活的真諦
他們令你手心冒汗
早晨你
看見父慈子孝的人
看見舉案齊眉的人
聽見充滿生活氣息的車流聲
而你更愛早餐店裏
和你一樣形單影隻的人
在彌漫的節日空氣中
錯落有致
孤單
相信我
如果你足夠清醒
終將被世界所拋棄
就像你早已拋棄這世界

2018.2.6.　　於 廣州

A Day in Beijing

First sip in the morning was beer
and the second was cigarette
Took a shower
washed the underwear with hands
Made a bowl of instant noodles
the flavor of spicy and sour tonkotsu soup
Went downstairs
wanted to buy an extra-large hot Caffè latte
It was so windy
my hair was instantly messed up
No milk in the corner shop
bought some canned coffee
Already 12:00 noon
then I wrote and
read poetry for a while
also read a short story in between
Went to meet someone
we chatted for two hours
The central idea he conveyed—
the ultimate beliefs were only
love and freedom
Had dinner with someone else
who I've known for years
but don't see often
He's writing a screenplay recently
(a love story)
We talked long about writing
and talked long about sex and love
didn't come to much conclusion
At about eleven o'clock at night
we separated

I took a taxi back to my rented short-term apartment in Shuangjing
(雙井)
(I've moved out from my cousin's flat in Shunyi [順義])
had meaningless chats
with two contacts on WeChat
and said good night to each other
(Finally got over
the fear of sleeping alone
if just having a small light on)
Lying on bed, thought about this and that
and listened to Coldplay's *Yellow* for a while
fell asleep at some point
(at least after 3:00am)

6th.Apr.2018.　　　　in Beijing

北京一日

早晨第一口是啤酒
第二口是香煙
洗澡
用手搓洗內褲
沖一碗泡面
酸辣豚骨口味的
下樓去
買一杯超大尺寸熱拿鐵
風太大了
髮型瞬間淩亂
便利店裏沒有奶
買了罐裝咖啡

已是中午 12:00
寫了一會兒詩
讀了一會兒詩
中間還讀了個短篇
去見一個人
我們聊了兩個小時
他傳達的中心思想是
終極信仰只有
愛和自由
晚飯約了另一人
多年朋友
但不常見面
他最近在寫劇本
　（愛情故事）
我們聊了半天寫作
又聊了半天性和愛情
沒什麼結論
夜裏將近十一點
各自散去
我打車回到雙井的短租房
　（我已從順義的表姐家搬出）
微信上和兩個人
東拉西扯
互道晚安
　（終於克服了
一個人睡覺的恐懼
只要亮一盞小燈在旁）
躺在床上東想西想
還聽了會兒 Coldplay 的 Yellow
不知道什麼時候睡了過去
　（起碼是凌晨三點之後了）

2018.4.6.　　　　於 北京

Eraser

Some say
why can't they be
gently wiped off like they were spider silk?
Wipe off then.
Like the long hair I'm dyeing right now
turning the deep, dark
black
into bright yellow
(even if it's only the superficiality of the world)
like the cigarette
I'm smoking meanwhile
I breathe out to it
its ashes fly and it dies out soon
and I would
neither cry, nor laugh
It should be done this way
To take a little courage–
it's nothing more than aiming at the heart
and stab it once more

8th.Mar.2018.   in Guangzhou

橡皮

有人說

為什麼不能把它們
當作蛛絲一樣輕輕抹去？
那就抹去。
像我此刻在染的長髮
把深不見底的
黑
變成明媚的黃
　（哪怕只是世界的表象）
像我同時在抽的
一支煙
我吹一口氣
它就灰飛煙滅
而我
不哭，也不笑
應當這樣做到
拿出一點兒勇氣
無非是對準心臟
再戳一刀

2018.3.8.　　　　於 廣州

Paramour

I should get used to solitude
like getting used to a paramour
lingering
bringing about the most profound orgasms
Solitude enters me
as a blast of gas in cone-shape

with the recoil of an assault rifle
I shudder for it
The icy solitude
the fiery solitude
the raging storms
and quiet down
My face aged, my body withered
like a candle flickering in wind
I embrace loneliness as I drift to sleep
Silver verses flash in my chaotic mind:
'A path emerges in the darkness'
'It's not the direction you seek'

21st.Nov.2017.   in Shenzhen

情人

我應該習慣孤獨
像習慣一個情人
纏綿悱惻
帶來最深刻的高潮
孤獨進入我
是一股錐狀氣體
衝鋒槍般的後坐力
我為之顫慄
冰冷的孤獨
火熱的孤獨
狂風驟雨
平息

面龐蒼老，形容枯槁
風中殘燭的我
懷抱孤獨入眠
混沌的腦中閃現銀白的詩行：
 "黑暗中出現一條路"
 "它不是你要找尋的方向"

2017.11.21.　於 深圳

Orchid H.

Receiving a notice for
a half-month business trip in the office
his first thought was of her
He tore off
a company letterhead
wrote down: Orchid.

I followed him
through twists and turns
to an old tube-shaped building
where I saw this woman
looked like a young wife to someone
and learned her full name:
Orchid H.

A sharp knife suddenly pierced my back
bottom to top
cold as

a Japanese seppuku
Before I could turn to see the assailant
I woke up
It was 5:59am

I didn't tell him (sleeping beside me)
about seeing my own death
but only mentioned
that he had a mistress in my dream named
'Orchid H.'
He sat up from the bed
said, huh
and walked into the shower room

11th.May.2018.   in Shenzhen

賀曉蘭

在辦公室接到通知要出差半月
他想到的第一個人
是她
隨手扯出
印有公司抬頭的信紙
寫下：蘭

我跟蹤他
七拐八拐走了很遠
一幢陳舊的筒子樓裏
看見了這個

有點兒像少婦的女人
得知她全名：
賀曉蘭

一把尖刀突然刺入我背後
由下至上
冰冷劃過
好似日本人的切腹
未及回頭看清兇手
醒了
清晨 5:59

我沒告訴身旁的他
看見了自己的死亡
只說
夢裏他有了一個情人叫
賀曉蘭
他從床上坐起來
嘿了一聲
走進洗手間

2018.5.11.　　　　於 深圳

Wilderness

Mountains of boulders
waters were cascading down

In the distance, a huge piece of dark cloud
drew close
The black curtain was covering
You were walking alone
on the rugged mountain roads
Vast darkness was enveloping you
Cold wind whistled by
and there were screeches of mountain birds
Against the pitch-black sky
large white characters suddenly emerged:

YOU—SEEK—THE—LORD'S—GRACE !

7th.Jan.2018.　　　　　in Xiamen

荒野

巨石之山
水飛流直下
遠處一片碩大烏雲
逐漸靠近
黑色幕布遮蓋
妳獨自一人
行走在崎嶇山路
浩瀚的黑暗將妳籠罩
冷風呼嘯而過
還有山鳥的尖叫
漆黑的天幕
白色大字驟然顯現:

妳
呼
求
主
！

2018.1.7. 　　　　於 廈門

Look, elder sister, there's a dead man over there!

An ancient stone building
with crumbling and worn pillars reaching out to the sky
People were bustling about
as if they had just finished some kind of bazaar
A boy, around five or six years old
ran up to you, pushed you:
Look, elder sister, there's a dead man over there!
His face was quirky with excitement
Your face suddenly paled
you turned to leave
The boy stopped you when you reached downstairs
He had used the innocent-look of a child
to convince your aunt
He found your aunt
out of nowhere
And your parents came too
you all sat around a small rectangular table
Your aunt was anxious, looked concerned

trying to lecture you
Everyone thought you were sick, and needed help
because you looked panicked
like a criminal fugitive
The boy sneaked around
making faces at you
fished out a wooden slingshot from his pocket
made a gesture to aim at you
and gave a fake 'pop'
You were upset, angry and scared
wanted to speak
but your throat was like blocked by poison
and couldn't make a sound at all
When you were finally able to speak
you could only yell one sentence over and over again
nothing else
You made random gestures on your forehead with one hand
saying only this one sentence—
'Your eyes are not my eyes!'

'Your eyes are not my eyes!'
'Your eyes are not my eyes!'

27th.Nov.2017.　　　　in Shenzhen

姐姐，你看，那邊有一個死人！

一幢古舊的石樓
有殘缺磨損的沖天柱子

人們熙熙攘攘
好像剛進行完什麼集會
一個大約五、六歲的男孩
沖到妳面前，推搡妳:
姐姐，你看，那邊有一個死人!
他臉上是古靈精怪的興奮
妳驟然變色
轉身就走
跑到樓下又被男孩攔下
他利用孩童的天真
說服了妳的姑媽
他不知從哪里
找來了妳的姑媽
你的父母也來了
你們圍坐在長方形小桌旁
姑媽焦急，神色關切
苦口婆心說教妳
大家認為妳病了，需要幫助
因為妳看上去慌慌張張
像個逃犯
男孩在一旁
偷著朝妳做鬼臉
從口袋裏摸出一把木制彈弓
做出樣子描准妳
又虛假地"啪"地一彈
妳又急又氣又害怕
想說話
嗓子卻像被毒藥給堵住
無論如何發不出聲音
等妳終於能夠發出聲音
妳反反復復竟只能喊出一句話
別的統統不行
一只手在額前胡亂比劃
就這一句——

"你的眼睛不是我的眼睛！"

"你的眼睛不是我的眼睛！"
"你的眼睛不是我的眼睛！"

2017.11.27.　　　於 深圳

Father

I turned and ran
'I don't need you to send me off!'
'Leave me alone!'
You rushed up
gripping me desperately
I yelled for help
people were watching
You pounded me with your fists
hitting my face and neck
We struggled fiercely
I fought to break free
and dashed into a small store across the street
slumping down on a seat
'Take your troubles outside...'
the shopkeeper's voice was faint
'He's harassing me!'
I gasped for breath
'Then call the police...'
'Fine, I'm calling the police!'
You snatched my phone away

'This phone, I bought it!'
'I'll pay you back!'
We got tangled up again
Fighting...
...
Eventually, I escaped
jumped into a taxi
You grabbed the door
'You'll go mad again,
and I'll have to take you to the hospital!'
'None of your business, even if I go mad!'
'Drive, drive!'
My voice was hoarse
The driver hit the accelerator
speeding away

12th.Mar.2018.   in Shenzhen

父親

我轉身跑
"我不要你送！"
"我自己走！"
你沖上來
拼命抱住我
我大喊救命
人們圍觀
你拿拳頭捶打
我的臉和脖子

我們糾纏了好一陣子
拼命掙脫你
我沖進對面的小賣部
一屁股坐下
"你們要搞事情出去搞……"
店老闆聲音很小
"他糾纏我！"
我喘著粗氣
"那你報警……"
"好我報警！"
你一把搶過我手機
"你手機都是我買的！"
"我還錢給你！"
我們又扭打在一起
……
……
最終我跑了
跑上一輛計程車
你把著門
"回頭你瘋了，還不得我帶你去醫院！"
"我瘋了也不要你管！"
"開車開車！"
我嗓子都啞了
司機一腳油門
揚長而去

2018.3.12.　　　　於 深圳

Your Footsteps

You came home
kicking over the trash bin as you entered
strode quickly to your desk
lit a cigarette
frowning deeply
Day after day
you're engulfed in video games
Tonight, I drifted into sleep
amidst the clacking sound of your keyboard
In this restless night
you lay beside me, fiddling with your mobile phone
Its screen casting a ghostly green glow in the dark
And you'd gotten up more times than
I could remember
even grabbing a beer from the fridge at 3:00am
gulping it down noisily
Only in moments of distraction
did I briefly fall into light sleep
I don't know what you're suffering from
whether you're tired of our life together
Before I fell asleep
you gritted your teeth and said
'I will get out of this place!'
To leave everything here behind
To leave
the mother tongue I so dearly love
For ten whole years
for the sake of my love for you
I've trudged mountains and crossed rivers
following you
like a piece of gum stuck to your shoe, cannot be shaken off

239th

Can I still keep up with
your stubborn footsteps this time?

1st.Dec.2017.   in Shenzhen

你的腳步

你回家了
進門時踢倒垃圾桶
疾速踱到書桌旁
點燃一支煙
眉頭緊鎖
日復一日地打遊戲
今晚我在你
劈裏啪啦按鍵盤的聲音中
輕輕入眠
這個輾轉反側的夜裏
你躺在我身邊擺弄手機
黑暗中發出綠色幽光
你又起身了許多次
數不清多少次
甚至從深夜三點的冰箱裏
抓出一瓶啤酒
咕咚咕咚灌進口中
只在一走神的時候
輕輕睡眠了一小會兒
我不知道你有什麼苦楚
是否已經厭倦與我的生活
在我入睡以前

你咬牙切齒地說:
"我要離開這地方！"
離開這裏的人和事物
離開
我所熱愛的母語
整整十年
為了愛你
我跋山涉水緊隨在你身後
像一塊甩也甩不掉的口香糖
這一次我還能不能
跟上你執拗的腳步

2017.12.1.　　　於 深圳

What Did You Do Today?

Woke up, ate, watched TV...
Oh, and took a dump

Well, no need to report that!

Because I spend long to take a dump
usually 30~50 minutes
It's a big part of my afternoon activity!

To brew tea, surf the web
on my phone, to play mobile games
during pooping

241st

You don't know
when I was in my previous company
upon hearing I was going to the toilet
my colleagues would shout:
Eh, wait a minute, wait a minute!
Shawn's going to poop, eh...
Whoever wants to pee? Hurry up!

6th.Apr.2018.   in Beijing

你今兒幹嘛了

起床，吃飯，看電視……
哦，還大了個便

得，這就不用匯報了

因為我大便時間比較長
通常需要 30-50 分鐘
是我下午的一項重要活動

醞釀，拿著手機
上網，打遊戲

你可不知道
過去我在公司裏
同事一聽我要上廁所
紛紛大喊
誒 等會兒等會兒
瀟子要大便了誒

誰要撒尿趕緊的

2018.4.6.　　　　於 北京

A Drinking Event

It was almost 5:00pm
when I asked Shawn out for a drink

He said, very much broke recently
don't want to go out

Discussed for a while
he said let's meet in his home

I was told there were dumplings for one person there
(Shawn: You'll have them!)

and half a bottle of baijiu (Chinese spirits)
(Shawn: Just drink whatever.)

How about I bring some food over?
Up to you, I'm good either way.

I've also been very much broke lately
so I bought

a bottle of Erguotou (Chinese spirits), cost 15 yuan

and a KFC family bucket

Navigated my way there
he opened the door excitedly:

'Ha, you've found it!
Such a strong girl? Why didn't you just call me to pick you up?'

12th.Apr.2018.　　　　in Beijing

酒局

下午快五點
我喊瀟子出來喝酒

"太窮了最近,
不想出門兒。"

商量半天
他喊我去他家

據說家裡有一人份的餃子
　(瀟子：給你吃!　)

還有半瓶白酒
　(瀟子：瞎逼喝唄。)

要不我帶點兒吃的過來?
隨你, 反正我純隨便。

最近我也特窮
就買了

十五元的二鍋頭
肯德基全家桶

按導航找過去
他眉飛色舞打開門

呵，挺能找呀!
特獨立? 也不知道給我打一電話?

2018.4.12.   於 北京

Youth II.

We four had drunk six bottles of red wine
today, slower and less than usual
Past 2:00 a.m.
my eyelids were at war
I dozed off, face down on the dining table
Bobby was yelling next to me
'Girl, don't fall asleep!
Or we all might as well!'

What had we been chatting about?
Seemed we talked for a while
about movies and video games

Shawn was all animated, telling his tales
about pooping and him with prostitutes
Meanwhile, Fan, barefoot
stood on the now unheated tiles
cursing, damn, it's fricking cold!
Out of the blue, Shawn asked him
'What's my signature song?'
Fan founded him both funny and annoying
'That "you want a home"?'
('A place not too big…'
from the song 'I Want a Home'《我想有個家》)

2005 was just like this
and it's still the same now
I got married
Bobby got married
but we stay the same
(Bobby yelled, 'What's the difference
whether you're married or not, anyway?!')
Feeling a bit moved
I laid my head on the dining table
and unknowingly fell asleep

7th.Apr.2018.   in Beijing

青春 II

四人喝掉六瓶紅酒
今天喝得慢且少
夜裏兩點多

我上下眼皮直打架
趴在餐桌上迷糊
Bobby 在一旁喊
妞兒　別睡呀
要睡可就都睡啦

我們都聊了些什麼？
好像聊了會兒
電影和遊戲
瀟子還眉飛色舞講了半天
他嫖娼和大便的故事
一旁帆子赤著腳
踩在剛沒了地暖的瓷磚上
喊著賊雞巴涼
瀟子冷不丁兒問他
我的成名曲是什麼？
帆子哭笑不得
"你想有個家？"
（"一個不需要多大的地方……"）

2005 年就是這樣
現在還這樣
我結婚了
Bobby 也結了
仍舊這樣
（Bobby 大叫：
你丫結婚了和沒結有什麼區別！）
我有點感動地
趴在餐桌上
不知不覺睡著了

2018.4.7.　　　於　北京

247th

Water

I've seen clean water
that washes away dust off bodies

I've seen dirty water
that was mixed with leftovers

flowing in twists and turns
between gaps of stone roads

stinking of rottenness
suffocating

I am astonished at the two
forms of water I've ever seen

Hard to believe, they actually
come from the same source

18th.Dec.2017.   in Shenzhen

248th

水

我見過清潔的水
洗淨周身污垢

我見過骯髒的水
混雜殘羹剩菜

在馬路的石縫間
曲裏拐彎流淌

發出腐朽惡臭
令人窒息

我驚訝於我所見過的
這兩種形態的水

難以置信，它們
竟來自同一源頭

2017.12.18.　　　於 深圳

My Sobriety Experiment

15 days ago, I vowed to quit drinking for a month
15 days later, I'd got drunk twice
The first time on 250-gram of Scotch whiskey
I ended up calling A an asshole
(though I'd been wanting to give him a piece of my mind)
The second time on 250-gram of 江小白
('Jiang Xiaobai', Chinese spirits)
pouring out my heart to B
(and waking up I kinda regretted it)

M. said
'Your poetry doesn't reveal much emotion'

Well, like the poor yearning for wealth
I guess I wish I were
a cold-blooded hitman
or maybe a solitary mountain

As for drinking less
it seems unfair to blame it all on the booze

24th.May.2018.   in Shenzhen

我的戒酒生涯

15 天前我決心戒酒一個月
15 天後我喝醉了兩次
第一次是半斤蘇格蘭威士卡
酒後把 A 給罵了
　(雖說我早想罵他)
第二次是半斤江小白
抓著 B 說了一堆真心話
　(起床時我有點後悔)

小木說
你詩裏看不出太多情緒

就像窮人希望自己有錢
我大概希望自己像個
冷面殺手
或者一座孤山吧

至於酒要不要少喝呢
好像也不能全賴酒

2018.5.24.　　　於 深圳

We Agreed to Jump off the Building Together

And I jumped
you didn't
This time
the fly was so long, and felt so real
the fall was so long, felt so real
The speed and coolness of wind passed through my body
I whimpered and shook my head, unable to make a sound
thinking of, you, who were still on the rooftop
This time
D
E
A
T
H
was so long, felt so real

Waking up
darkness
The air was heavy on my chest, and I couldn't move
Beside, you were fast asleep

7th.Nov.2017.   in Shenzhen

我們說好要一起跳樓

我縱身一躍
你沒有下來
這一次
飛翔如此漫長，如此逼真
下墜如此漫長，如此逼真
風的速度和涼意穿過我身體
我嗚嗚晃著腦袋發不出聲音
想著，還在樓頂的你
這一次
死
｜
亡
如此漫長，如此逼真

醒來
漆黑
空氣沉甸甸壓在我胸口，不能動彈
一旁，你熟睡

2017.11.7.　　　　　於 深圳

I Hate Liars

Can't imagine their lives
The thought of basing a life on lies is beyond me

253rd

They invalidate my imagination
I need to envision the real
Or rather
the reality in my imagination must be grounded in truth
instead of living in a masturbatory fantasy
It's a gripping feeling—
it brings my feet back to the ground
steadies my breath

22nd.Nov.2017.　　　　in Shenzhen

我討厭說謊的人

無法想像他們的生活
我無法基於謊言去想像一個人的生活
他們令我的想像力變得無效
必須想像真實
或者說
想像中的真實必須基於真實而存在
而非活在自慰般的假想中
一種攥緊的感覺——
它令我的雙腳回到地面
平穩呼吸

2017.11.22.　　　於 深圳

I'm on Water

Floating on water like a baby
limbs splayed, on my back
not sinking
The sky envelops me
The sun's absent
but still bright and dazzling
I sleep
with my eyes closed tightly
A cold wind blows in my chaotic dreams
Yet, it's not cold enough
The weather is not cold enough
it can be colder
Coldness makes me sharp
even in dreams
filled with power of sorrow

25th.Nov.2017.   in Shenzhen

我在水上

如同嬰兒一般浮在水上
四肢叉開，仰面朝天
並不下沉
天空將我包圍

太陽缺席
然而依舊光亮奪目
我雙目緊閉
睡眠
混沌的夢中有冷風吹過
然而還不夠冷
天氣還不夠冷
可以再寒冷一些
寒冷使我凜冽
即便是在夢中
充滿悲傷的力量

2017.11.25.　　　　於　深圳

Untitled

1.
I seek for beauty that doesn't exist in this world
for which I'm often defeated
Half of me is always against the other half
like
the body not letting go of the soul
the heart versus the mind
Inability to know
or come close to myself
The two poles of the magnetic field
Those with the answers are all at the masquerade
the hippies are long gone
my grief is absolute

On a night when tears flowed like springs, someone said to me:
'Impurity is justified.'
Suffering and agony—
such words shouldn't be mentioned
Fate has its own decree

2.
Today I've listened intently to a song
titled *Young and Beautiful*
年輕與美貌
Will you still love me
when I'm no longer, young and beautiful
Will you still love me
when I got nothing, but
my aching soul? The song sings
Sometimes it's hard for me to concentrate
my heart is flooded with inexplicable sadness
like a layer of undertone
like when you have penetrated a secret of the humankind
—that sad

3
I was walking on the long concrete path in the community
Behind me, the crackling sound of footsteps
rapid, like someone running fast
I turned around
no trace of any person anywhere
only a narrow path, stretching into the distance

4
In a way
I start to understand Zuo Qin's (左秦) death
(a young poet, a acquaintance who killed himself)
and start to understand Hai Zi (海子), Van Gogh, Plath...

It's not that lacking people who love you
nor that they love you insincerely
It's just all those survival skills
those comforting words and actions—
they lose effectiveness when it really matters
You sink alone into a bottomless black hole
swirling downwards
pitch black, that you can't even see your fingers

5
Life is so meaningless, yet I can't bear to die
Feng (小鳳) says to me:
'Sister, come to eat fish at my place'
People are trying to love you
in one way or another
but you're beyond saving
As a matter of fact, only you
could save yourself
(What a cliche
yet how true)

Feb.~Mar.2018.   in Guangzhou, Changsha, Shenzhen

無題

1.
我追尋不存在於這世界之美
為此時常失魂落魄
我的一半始終對抗另一半
就像

肉體不放過靈魂
心與腦的較量
無法認識
或靠近自己
磁場的兩極
持有答案者都在化妝舞會上
嬉皮士已經死去
我的悲傷很徹底
淚如泉湧的夜晚，有人對我說
不純粹的才是好的!
不應提到受苦受難
這樣的字眼
命運自有定數

2.

今天我專注地聽過一首歌
歌名是 Young and Beautiful
年輕與美貌
當我年華不再，容顏老去
當我一無所有，只剩下
疼痛的靈魂，你是否
愛我如初。歌裏唱。
有時我很難專注
心裏泛著莫名的傷感
像一層底色
像你參透了人類的秘密
那樣傷感

3

我在社區長長的水泥路上走
背後傳來劈啪的腳步聲
疾速，像一個人在奔跑
回轉身
萬徑人蹤滅

只有小路，伸向遠方

4
某種程度上
我理解了左秦的死
(我認識的一位年輕詩人，他自殺身亡)
理解了海子，梵高，普拉斯……
不是缺少愛你的人
也並非他們愛得不真摯
只是那些求生技能
那些勸慰的話語和行動
在關鍵時候都失去了作用
你獨自陷入無底黑洞
朝下漩渦
伸手不見五指

5
生命是如此無意義，我卻捨不得去死
小鳳說：
妹妹，來姐姐這兒吃魚吧。
人們都在愛你
以這樣那樣的方式
而你無藥可救
能救你的只有
你自己
　(多麼俗套的一句話
卻又多麼正確)

2018.2.~3.　　　於 廣州，長沙，深圳

Weariness

Sometimes I feel tired of everything
Writing feels pointless
Poetry feels pointless
Everything feels just pointless
I even think
maybe death would be a relief—
an end to it all
Yet, I lack the courage
to die
can't even get that right
And then there are also so many
who claim to 'love you'
Now I remember my depression
at its worst—
how strong that will to live was:
just wanting to survive
to keep going
to create
to love
I should cling to that feeling
I don't know how
to perk myself up
Maybe I should just let loose
totally and utterly
A downward force, a spell
to feel an extraordinary thrill
And right now
I stand in a dark-blue long dress
at a bookstore's entrance
Standing
calmer than anyone else

smoking,
watching the smoke rings
drift away into the distance

13th.Nov.2017.   in Shenzhen

厭倦

有時我對一切感到厭倦
寫作也沒什麼意思
詩歌也沒什麼意思
一切都沒勁
我甚至想
大概死了會好
一了百了
然而我還沒有
死亡的勇氣
連死亡
我也沒有幹成
何況還有那麼多
所謂愛我的人
又想起憂鬱症
病發最嚴重時——
那時的求生欲多強啊
就只想活下去
活下去
去創造
去愛
我應當死死記住那種感覺
我不知道該怎麼

讓自己打起精神來
或許該鬼混一番
徹底的鬼混
一種向下的力量，魔法
獲得超凡脫俗的快感
此刻
我身穿一襲深藍長裙
在書店樓下站著
站著
比任何人更沉靜
抽煙
看煙圈縹緲
飄向遠方

2017.11.13.　　　於 深圳

Cinema

When there's nothing to do
I head to the cinema
alone
just me, to the cinema
I've seen 'Seventy-Seven Days'
about a young man crossing the no-man's land of Qiangtang (羌塘),
Tibet
I've seen 'Murder on the Orient Express'
about a murder, and revenge
Also, a film I can't recall the name of, about a global disaster
that was spectacularly reversed by two supernatural brothers
blah, blah, blah

Walking on the way to the cinema
the air is slightly cool
A faint Latin music echoes in the distance
its pulsating beats emphasize my loneliness
Yet this loneliness is comfortable
almost a variant of freedom
When there's nothing to do
I head to the cinema
alone, just me
where a movie ticket is an expense I can afford
seeking solace in material things
I feel warm and safe

22nd.Nov.2017.   in Shenzhen

電影院

無事可做時
我就去電影院
獨自一人
去電影院
看過《七十七天》
講一個男人穿越西藏羌塘無人區的故事
看過《東方快車謀殺案》
關於謀殺，復仇
還有一部想不起名字的電影，講全球災難
被神奇兩兄弟驚天逆轉
等等，等等
走在去電影院的路上
天氣微涼

不遠處傳來隱約的拉丁舞曲
跳躍的鼓點強調了我的孤獨
然而這孤獨又是愜意的
仿佛也是自由的變體
無事可做時
我就去電影院
獨自一人
電影票是我能承受的消費
在物質中尋求安慰
我感到溫暖，安全

2017.11.22.　　　　於 深圳

Untitled

Strip off my clothes, layer by layer
like peeling an onion
until naked
Then walk into the streets, into the city
wandering amidst towering skyscrapers
on rough concrete paths
They are no different
from a secluded valley
My bare feet are pierced by glass
shards embedded in flesh
Ignoring the astonished stares
of passersby, and the pain
bleeding
And so, I walk, far and long
all the way to the church

29th.Dec.2017.　　　　in Shenzhen

無題

將我的衣服一件件剝落
像剝一顆洋蔥
直到赤裸
然後去大街，去城市
在摩天大廈之間
坑窪的水泥路面徘徊
它和與世隔絕的山谷
並無什麼兩樣
一雙赤腳被玻璃紮破
碎片嵌在皮肉裏
我忽略人們詫異的
目光，以及疼痛
血流不止
就這樣走了很遠
一直到教堂

2017.12.29.　　於 深圳

Postscript:

May Stars Shine upon You

by Xi Nan

It had always been a wish of mine to publish a book of selected poems written over the past fourteen years. I feel very happy to have made it really happen this time.

2005 was the year when I wrote the first poem in my life. I was an undergraduate student in the UK and was about to graduate from university, and at that time, my relationship with my boyfriend was not going well, and I had a lot of emotions building up in my heart. One day at my internship, after I had finished my work for the day, I was dazed in my seat, looking out of the window at the very rare sunshine in England, suddenly picked up a pen for some reason I didn't know, and wrote down my first poem, 'Samsara', on a blank piece of paper in front of me. And that poem is also included in this collection.

Looking back, my initial foray into poetry was without any specific aim. Over time, however, poetry became a regular way of expressing my inner and emotional world.

Thus, as mentioned above, most of my early poems (for a long time) were not given much deliberation and were only a way of catharsis. In the middle period, because of severe bipolar disorder, I could barely write at one point, and when I did, the things I wrote could hardly please myself (yet I'm still grateful for poetry—it has accompanied me through almost all the darkest moments of my life). At another time, I was fascinated by several poetry writing genres that emerged in China at the turn of the century, but later stopped liking them (and found some things in them weren't really for me). Finally, right now, in the second half of 2017, I seem to have finally moved out from my old writing stage and, to some extent, found a place in the new one. It can be said that during this period, my poetry writing has been influenced by the school of Chinese 'colloquial language poetry' (口語詩), but at the same time, I've learned the importance of maintaining my own independent thinking under the influence of the school.

From 2005 to 2018, all the selected poems are here (probably close to 200 poems? Or perhaps fewer?), submitted for your judgment. The journey from my earliest poetry to today's work has not been easy—I've trekked through fourteen long years, marked by many dark, sunless periods, as above mentioned.

Fortunately, I'm still alive, and haven't stopped writing. Just for these two facts alone, there's solace to be found. Writing is indeed one of the few things I've managed to maintain consistently throughout my life so far.

In the postscript of my last poetry collection, now seen by me as quite unsatisfactory, 'Everything Can Only Be This Way, But Creation Never Stops,' I once wrote the following passage:

'...In the early days of writing, I thought: One day, my words are *going to reach so many people and have such a profound impact... Much later, it seems that many writers have to accept certain inherent limitations... And now I am convinced that often, solitary writers are merely writing for one or two real readers. In those fleeting, special moments, you and I have shared a silent understanding. Thus, these unremarkable words I've written also hold the potential for a moment's validation.'*

To this day, the above thoughts of mine haven't changed. And even now, I remind myself: Writing should be a return to the initial aspiration. What is that 'initial aspiration'? I remember once in high school, I was required to participate in a provincial math competition (mandatory for everyone, bizarrely), and I couldn't understand the questions on the paper at all. It was a sweltering summer in Guangzhou outside the window, while inside, my classmates were buried in their work and exam, frantically writing answers. A very real sense of despair struck me in an instant. So, I coolly marked 'C' for all the multiple-choice questions (years later, hearing the song 'All Cs' [都選 C], it really resonated deeply with me), then handed in my paper and wandered onto the playground to space out... Reflecting on it, that might have been the moment I fell in love with writing.

Yes, back then, writing was merely a window for self-expression, and the readers who came and went were just a few close friends. Writing at that time was not for fame or fortune, not for the so-called 'networking'... I believe this is what my 'initial aspiration' was. People say that at a certain stage in life, one must learn to start subtracting, reducing until all that remains is a clean, refreshing self, only a heart with the 'initial aspiration.' This is my current writing passion.

I am grateful for those who have always been patient, tolerant, and caring towards me—they have enabled me to never stop loving and pursuing freedom truthfully; they have encouraged me to never stop writing and creating diligently and earnestly, even though such writings often don't reap much applause or flowers.

I'm grateful to Fish Lu, my life partner, my love, my mentor and best friend.

As always, I am also grateful to my readers (especially those who have reached this far): you have given my fragmented words unique meanings. May all readers gain something from this book.

I feel that when I am writing this 'Postscript', my mood is bright and upbeat, and the helplessness and despair that I felt when I wrote the postscript for my last poetry-collection in 2014 no longer exist. I've found a way to coexist with my mental illness, feeling both joy and gratitude. I thank God, my Heavenly Father.

May stars shine upon you.

27th.Jul.2017.   first draft in Guangzhou
7th.Jan.2021.   revised in Shaoxing, Zhejiang

[7th.Jan.2021. Addendum: In revising and organizing this manuscript, I revisited the arduous and solitary journey—a decade in a foreign land, amidst a non-native language environment—of my writing exploration before my temporary return to China in 2016. Post-2018, the evolution in my writing became increasingly pronounced. Thus, in the process of revising this book, in addition to adjusting some of my earlier works, I also added dozens of poems written in late 2017 and in 2018. They serve as the perfect epilogue to the lengthy 'early phase' of my personal writing journey. Looking forward, I aim to continue new creation and breakthrough—perhaps more for self-realization than for others. Lastly, consistent with what I wrote in the 'Postscript' above, I'm still learning the art of subtraction in my writing, hoping one day to distill it to the essence of 'nothing but love and creation, and submission to the laws of time' (as Fish Lu has put it)—a challenging lesson indeed, but one I'm committed to pursuing using a whole life time, with all my heart and strength.]

Dec.2018.   first draft in Guangzhou
7th.Jan.2021.   revised in Shaoxing, Zhejiang

後記:

願星光照耀你們

文/西楠

出版一本寫詩十四年來的精選集，一直是我的心願。這次能夠把這件事情做成，我感到非常快樂。

2005 年，是我寫下人生中第一首詩的一年。當時我在英國念本科，大學快畢業了，那時戀情不順，心中鬱積了許多情緒。一天在實習單位，當天的事情做完了，我在位置上發呆，看著窗外難得一見的英格蘭陽光，鬼使神差地拿起筆，就在面前的一張白紙上寫下了這第一首詩——《輪迴》。這首詩也被收錄在了這本選集當中。

現在想來，那時寫詩是沒有任何目的性的。到了後來，詩歌就成了我表現自己內心和情感世界的一個常規辦法。

所以，如上所述，我的早期詩歌 (很長一段時間) 大多沒有考慮太多，僅作宣洩的一種方式。到了中期，因為罹患嚴重的躁鬱症，曾經一度幾乎無法下筆，即使下筆，寫出的東西也十分難以取悅自己 (我仍感激詩歌——它幾乎陪伴我度過了生命中所有最黑暗的時刻)。另一段時間，我則迷上了本世紀初興起於中國的幾個詩歌寫作流派，但後來又不再喜歡（也發現了其中的一些東西，並不真正適合自己）。最後，就到了現在，2017 的下半年，我似乎終於脫離了自己舊的寫作階段，一定程度上，又在新的寫作階段中找到了位置。可以說，在這一時期，我的詩歌寫作受到中國"口語詩"流派影響較大，但同時又懂得了在流派影響下保持自身獨立思考的重要性。

2005 年到 2018 年，挑選出來的詩全在這裡了（可能有近 200 首？或者更少？），交由你們評判。從最初的詩歌寫作走到今天不易，我整整跋山涉水地走了十四年，並且，如同前文所提及，其中也包括許多暗無天日的時光。

還好，如今我仍然活著，並且沒有停止寫作——我想僅因為這兩點，已值得欣慰。寫作算是我長到這麼大，堅持得最好的事情之一了。

在我上一本現在看來差強人意的詩集的後記《一切只能如此，但永不停止創造》中，我曾經寫下這樣一段話：

"……寫作初期會想：有一天，我的文字要抵達那麼那麼多人，產生那麼那麼深遠的影響……很久以後看來，大概許多寫作者都不得不接受某些存在的局限性……如今我已確信，很多時候，孤獨的寫作者們不過是為那一、兩個真實存在的讀者而寫。在那些轉瞬即逝的特殊時刻，你我已有片刻心領神會，如此，我寫下的這些無甚新意的文字也有了瞬間有效的可能。"

我至今沒有改變以上想法。並且，如今我還告誡自己：寫作，應當回到初心。什麼是"初心"？我想起高中時有一次，被要求參加全省數學競賽（所有人必須參加，匪夷所思），根本看不懂題目。當時窗外是廣州悶熱的夏天，窗內是前後左右一個個埋頭苦幹、奮筆疾書的同窗。一種真切的絕望感瞬間擊中我。於是我酷酷地把選擇題全部選上了 C（多年以後偶然聽到《都選 C》這首歌，真是特別共鳴呀），然後交卷走到操場上發呆……想來，我就是那時候愛上寫作的吧。

是的，在那時，寫作只是自我宣洩的一扇窗口，來來去去的讀者也只有那幾個與我要好的朋友。那時的寫作，不為名利、不為圈子……我想，這就是我的"初心"吧。都說人生走到一定階段，便要學著開始做減法，減到最後，只剩下乾乾淨淨、清清爽爽的自己，只剩下：一顆初心。這就是我現階段的寫作願望。

我感謝那些始終待我耐心、寬容，關愛著我的人們——他們使我無論如何不曾停止真實地去愛、去追尋自由；使我無論如何不曾停止認真、勤奮地創作，哪怕這樣的文字時常並不能收穫太多鮮花和掌聲。

謝謝魯魚，我的人生伴侶、愛人和良師益友。

一如既往，我也感謝我的讀者們（特別是能夠讀到這裡的人）：是你們為我支離破碎的文字賦予了獨一無二的意義。願所有讀者均能從此書中有所獲得。

我感到，當我在寫作這篇"後記"時，我的心情是爽朗的、節奏是明快的。2014 年寫作上一本詩集"後記"時那樣無助、絕望的心情不復存在。我能夠與我的精神疾病共存了，感到快樂與感恩。感謝上帝，我的天父。

願星光照耀你們。

2017.7.27.　　初稿　於廣州
2021.1.7.　　　修訂　於浙江紹興

（**2021.1.7. 補記：** 重新修訂、整理這本書稿，看到了自己 2016 年回中國暫居以前，在異國非母語環境中艱難而孤獨的寫作探索，長達近十年之久。2018 年開始，我在寫作上的變化愈發明顯，因此在修訂本書的過程中，除去對一些前作的調整，也增補了數十首寫於 2017 年末和 2018 年的詩。用它們來作為我的整個個人寫作中，漫長的"早期"階段的尾聲，再適合不過。望在今後，我會繼續新的創造和突破——也許更多是對自我意義上的 [而不是為他人]，最後，與上面"後記"中所寫相同的是，至今我仍在學習給自己的寫作做減法，希望有朝一日會簡單到魯魚口中的"只剩下愛與創造，和對時間的順從"——這不是一門容易的功課，但我願意為之身體力行。）

2018.12.　　　　初稿　於廣州
2021.1.7.　　　修訂　於浙江紹興

Editor of this Book: Fish Lu
本書編輯：魯魚